John Cecil Stephenson

(1889-1965)

A Modernist in Hampstead

Burgh House

30 March - 18 September 2022

This catalogue is dedicated to Marjorie Guthrie

We would especially like to acknowledge the help of Caroline Maclean,
Conor Mullan, Peyton Skipwith, and the team at Burgh House:
Sophie Richards, Amber Turner, Mark Francis and Victor Hall

We would also like to thank:
Patrick Allman-Ward, Daniel Dullaway, Mark Francis, Jonathan Guthrie,
Sarah Guthrie, Geoff Hassell of Artbiogs.co.uk, Alex Lewis,
Eva Liss, Maudji Llewellyn, Stephen Maisel,
Filippo Fiorini Miotti, Tony Mould,
David Wade, Mark Wake
and Tom Wheare

First published in 2022 by LISS LLEWELLYN

ISBN : 978-1-9993145-6-9

Text © Michael Harrison, Paul Liss, Tony Mould & Peyton Skipwith

Photography: Glyn Clarkson, Pierre Emmanuel Coste &
Petra van der Wal

Design and Typesetting by David Maes
Printed by Zenith Media, February 2022

John Cecil Stephenson

(1889-1965)

A Modernist in Hampstead

Edited by Sacha Llewellyn, Paul Liss & George Richards

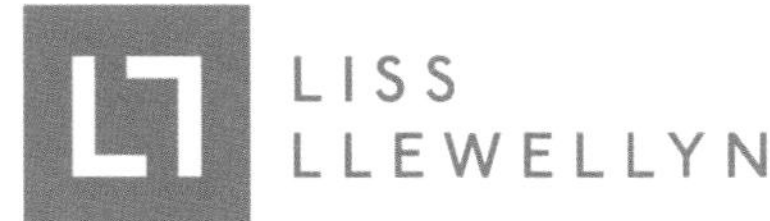

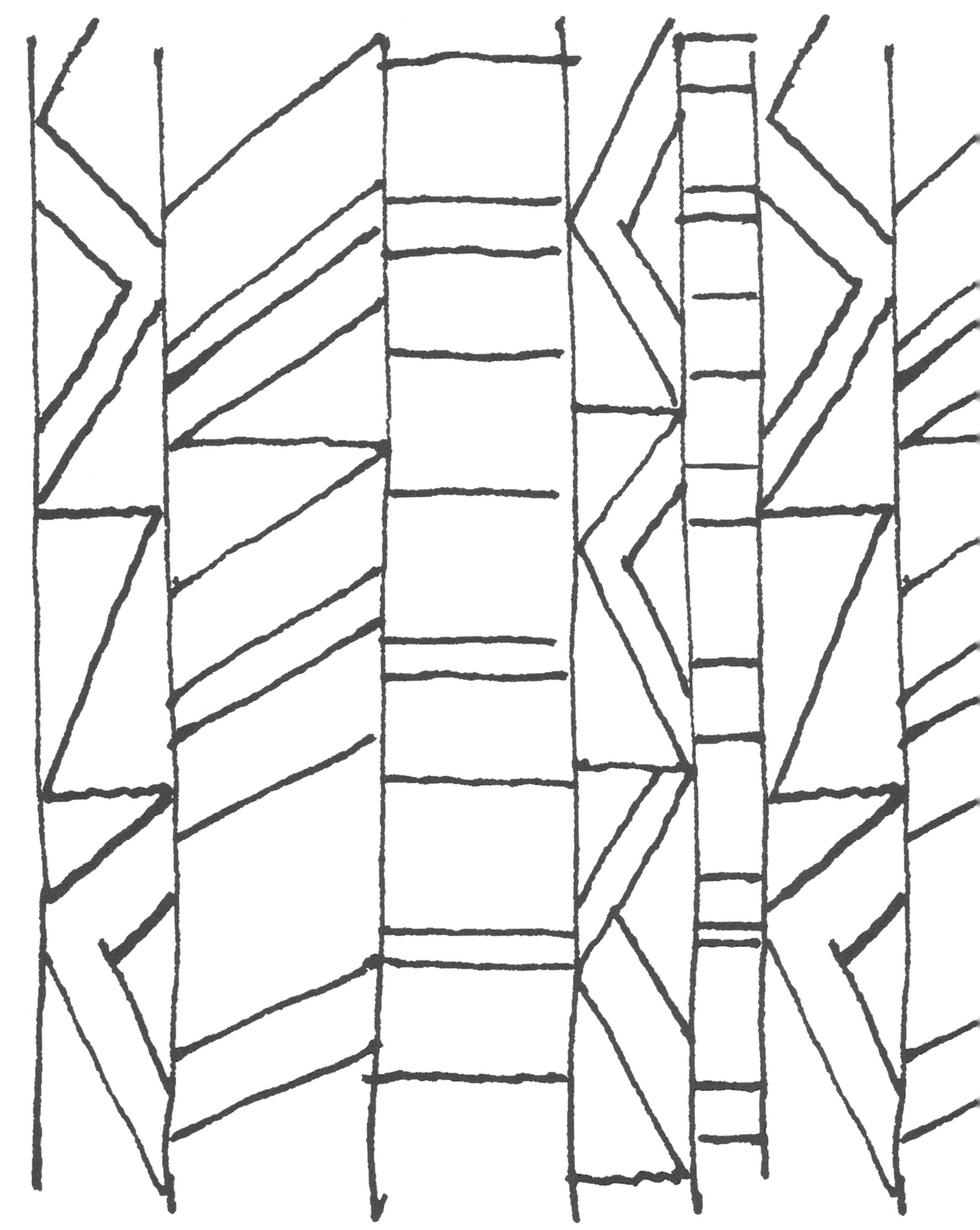

Contents

Acknowledgements   7
Paul Liss

Introduction – A Modernist in Hampstead   9
Paul Liss

Mall Studios, Hampstead   13
Michael Harrison

John Cecil Stephenson (1889-1965) – Pioneer of Abstraction   39
Peyton Skipwith

CATALOGUE

1930-1940   52
1940-1950   66
1950-1960   74

BIOGRAPHICAL NOTES   91

John Cecil Stephenson   94
Tony Mould

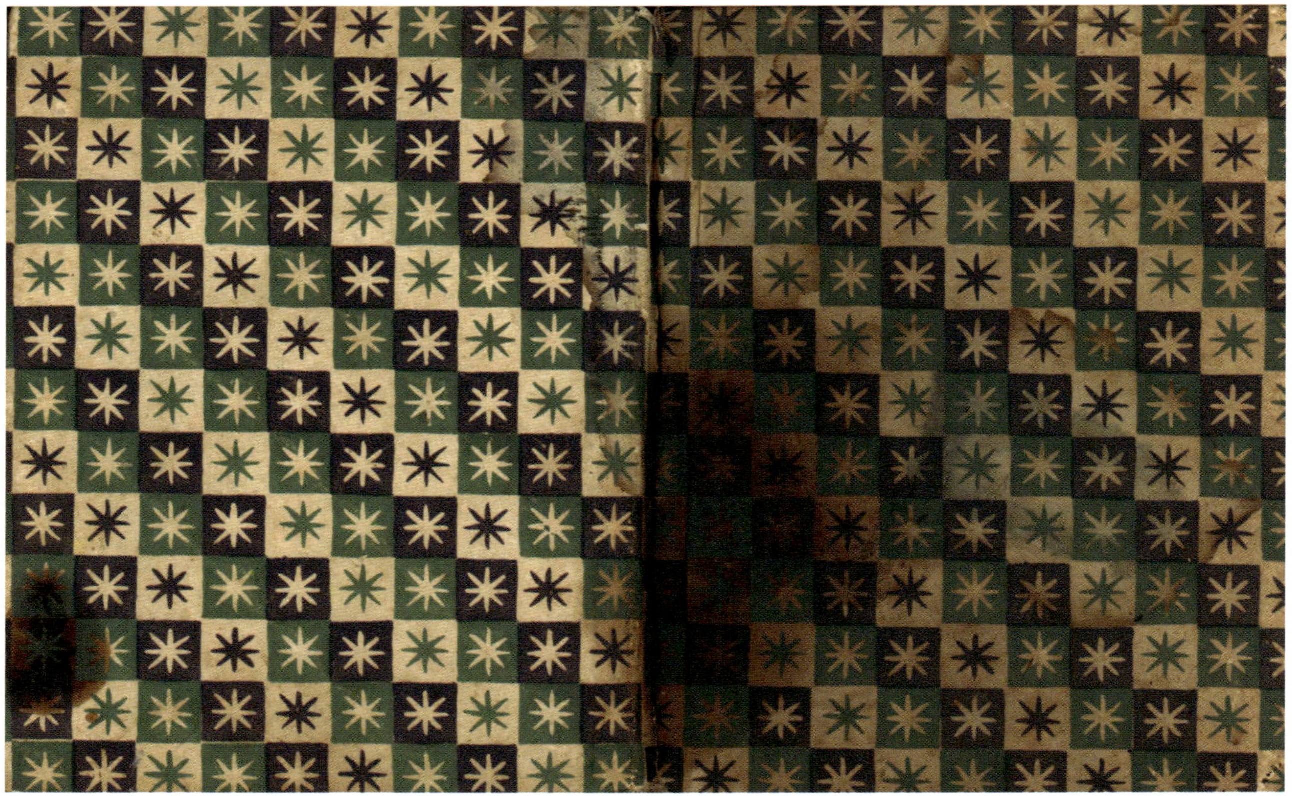

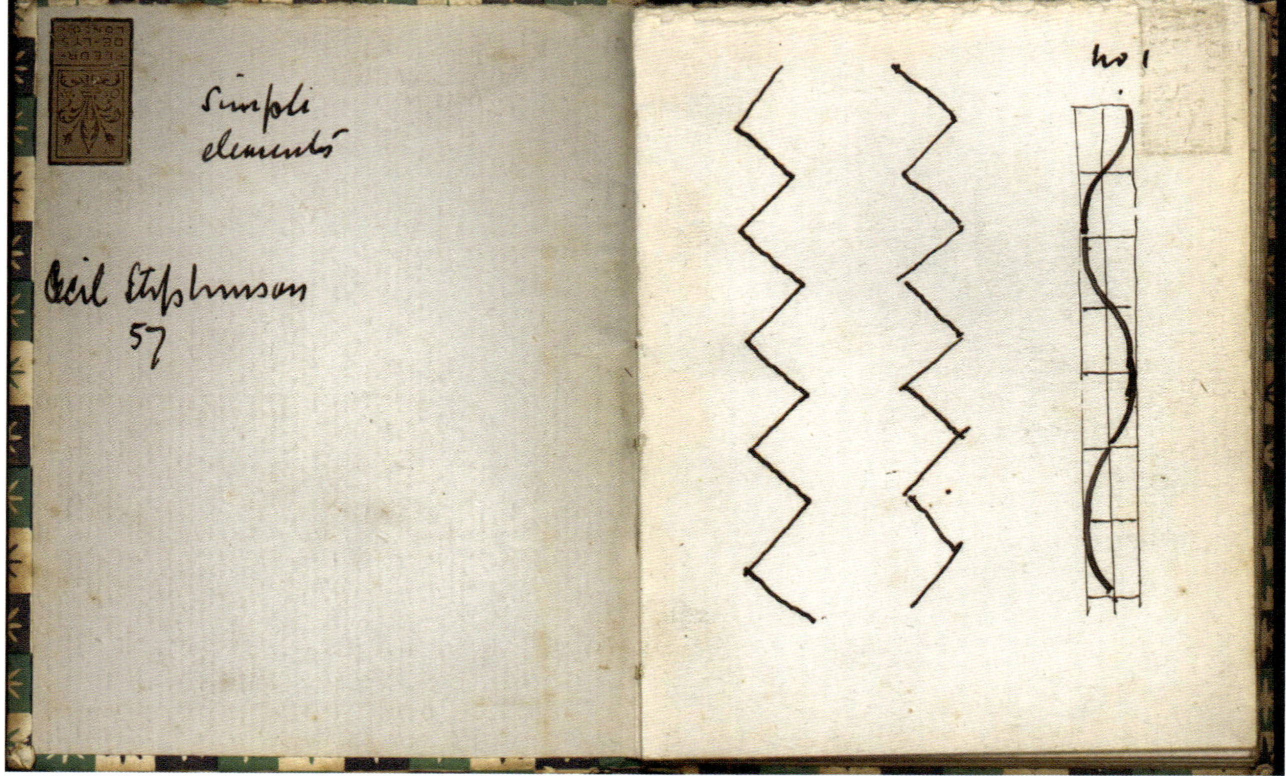

Cat. 1 – Sketchbook 'Simple Elements', 1957, signed, titled and dated on inside,
pencil, pen & ink and watercolour on paper, 5 ½ x 4 ¼ in. (14 x 11 cm). Provenance: The Artist's studio.

Acknowledgements

Paul Liss

There is something entirely satisfying about holding this exhibition at Burgh House in Hampstead: Stephenson lived at Mall Studios for half a century, from the time of the First World War until his death in 1966. There is thus a sense of coming home, a happy aligning of the stars. But this exhibition also has its origins in serendipity: 10 years ago I asked Michael Harrison, curator of Kettles Yard in Cambridge, to write an essay about Stephenson's life in Hampstead, with the intention of re-printing an expanded version of Simon Guthrie's invaluable, but out of print and largely black and white monograph: *Life and Art of John Cecil Stephenson: A Victorian Artist's Journey to Abstract Expressionism* (1997). Disappointingly, Michael replied that he was too busy (writing a monograph on Alan Reynolds); so I put the project to one side.

Two years later, much to my surprise, Michael contacted me: "It seems a little while since we were in touch about the introduction for the Stephenson book. As you haven't chased me, I hope I'm on schedule. I have written a piece which has turned out a good deal longer than you had anticipated. Read it and see whether you can use it. I shall be undergoing some medical treatment from next Thursday so, if any work is needed, it would be as well to do it in advance of that."

Tragically that was the last I heard from Michael — he passed away a few days later. His wonderful essay is published here for the first time.

Fate played a kinder hand two years ago when, out of the blue, I was contacted by a former student of Stephenson's, Tony Mould, who wanted to share an image of a painting, *Divertimento II*, that he had commissioned from Stephenson in 1955. A brief memoir by Tony is published at the end of this catalogue and we are delighted to exhibit for the first time this wonderful work (**CAT. 24**).

This exhibition includes many other works which are being seen in public for the first time since leaving the Mall Studios in Hampstead. The joy of curating an exhibition around work whose provenance has laid undisturbed since its creation is twofold: firstly there is the privilege of having access to major works that the artist deliberately retained — *Tonality* (**CAT. 27**), for instance, always hung in Stephenson's studio (**Fig. 29**), and provides a key link to understanding his journey towards Abstract Expressionism. There is also the opportunity to catch a glimpse of an artist's journey through preparatory works such as the tiny studio book (**CAT. 1**), illustrated opposite dating to 1957, entitled *Simple Elements*: in this it is almost as if Stephenson has coded his own artistic DNA across its 48 pages, offering an array of the underlying patterns from which he constructed his art.

We are grateful to Marjorie Guthrie, Stephenson's daughter-in-law to whom this catalogue is dedicated, and to her children Sarah and Jonathan Guthrie, without whose support this project would not have been possible.

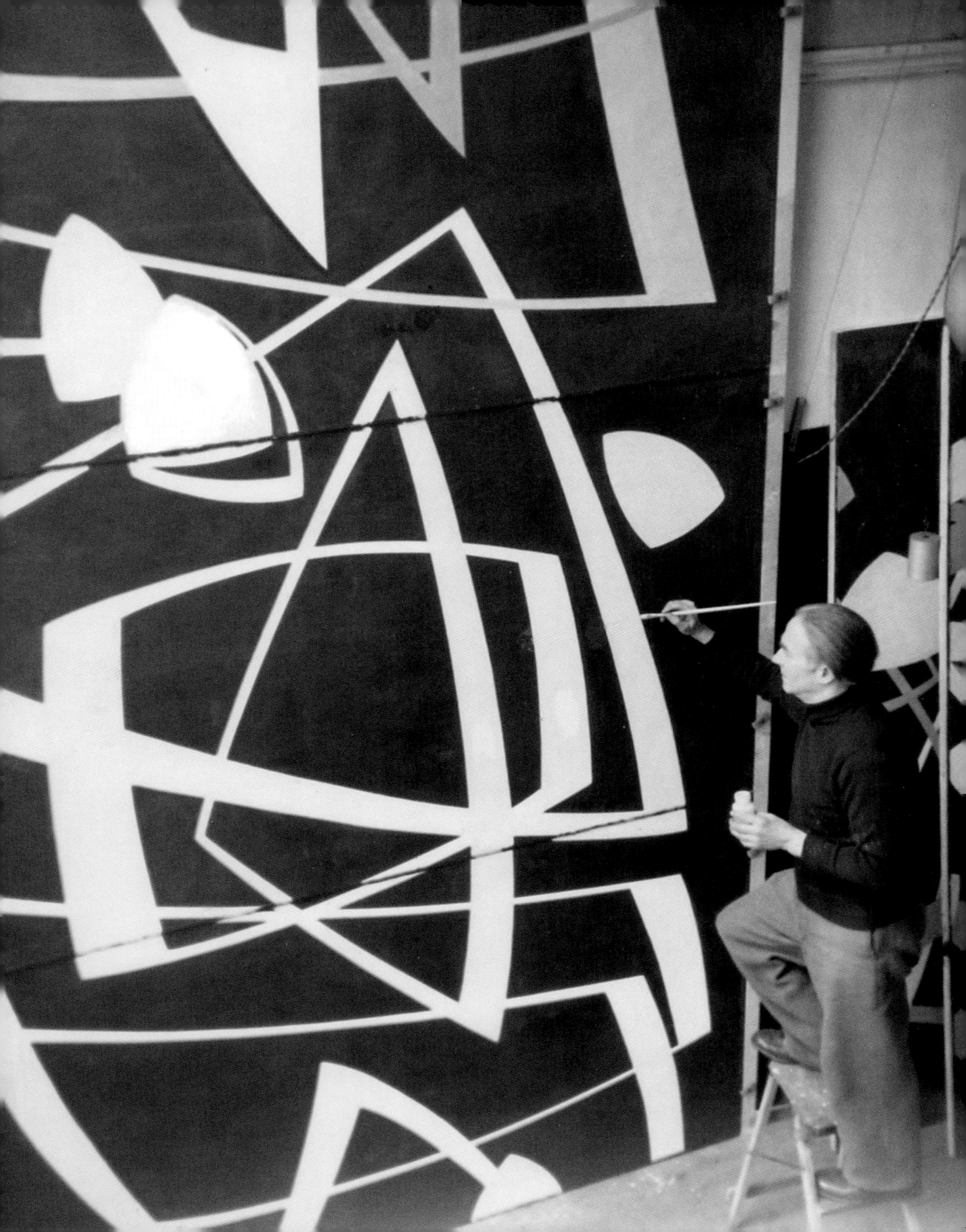

Introduction – A Modernist in Hampstead

Paul Liss

By the end of John Cecil Stephenson's art school training – first a scholarship to Leeds Art School then to The Royal College of Art – he was in a position to produce, in a professional capacity, still lives, landscapes and portraits. Like many painters of his generation, who had received similarly conventional instruction, he became a competent teacher, appointed in 1922, as Head of Art at The Northern Polytechnic. In this mould Stephenson might have remained a largely undistinguished painter – but in the early 1930s he found himself at the centre of a group of artists with *avant-garde* credentials, and his own art underwent a remarkable transformation. By 1934 he was exhibiting groundbreaking works such as *Mask* (**CAT. 7**), at the 7 & 5 Society, and in 1937 was a key contributor to the watershed publication and exhibition *Circle*, where his work was showcased alongside that of luminaries such as Kazimir Malevich, Le Corbusier, Fernand Léger, Alberto Giacometti and Pablo Picasso. What led Stephenson to become, in the words of the celebrated art critic Herbert Read, 'one of the earliest artists in the country to develop a completely abstract style'? His remarkable journey from figurative art to abstraction is brilliantly recounted in Peyton Skipwith's essay *John Cecil Stephenson, Pioneer of Abstraction.*

Between March 1919 and November 1965, John Cecil Stephenson lived in London at No. 6 Mall Studios, off Tasker Road, Hampstead. As the father figure of what Read christened 'a nest of gentle artists', his next door neighbours included, during the course of the decade leading up to WW2, Barbara Hepworth, John Skeaping, Ben Nicholson and Henry Moore. Such fertile ground was further enriched by visits from artists fleeing persecution – including Piet Mondrian, László Moholy-Nagy and Alexander Calder – just a few of the many internationally acclaimed artists who whilst passing through London formed part of the art set who congregated around Read's house at No. 3 Mall Studios.

Surprisingly, for an artist born in the last decade of the 19th century, Stephenson's energies were far from spent by the end of the Second World War. After a remarkably fertile return to figurative art during the war years (**CAT. 18 - 22**), his original quest for a pure form of abstraction entered a new and more ambitious phase. Of particular significance is *Tonality* (**CAT. 27**)described by Simon Guthrie as one of two major work produced in 1954, and which captures the transition that Stephenson's work underwent from hard edged abstraction to abstract expressionism: "The feeling of 'Tonality' is more schematic and light-hearted. An array of brightly coloured oblongs with little depth, produces a slightly similar effect to the arrays of vertical forms seen in the 30s pictures. To a small extent these works were a move away from the ultra hard-edge style'."   As the 1950s unfolded he completed a series of impressive large-scale murals for The Festival of Britain (1951), Solar House, (1956), Queen Mary's College, London, 1957, (**CAT. 4, 28**) and The Brussels Exposition (1958). Inspired by developments

Fig. 1 - Stephenson painting the flourescent mural for the Festival of Britain, April 5, 1951.

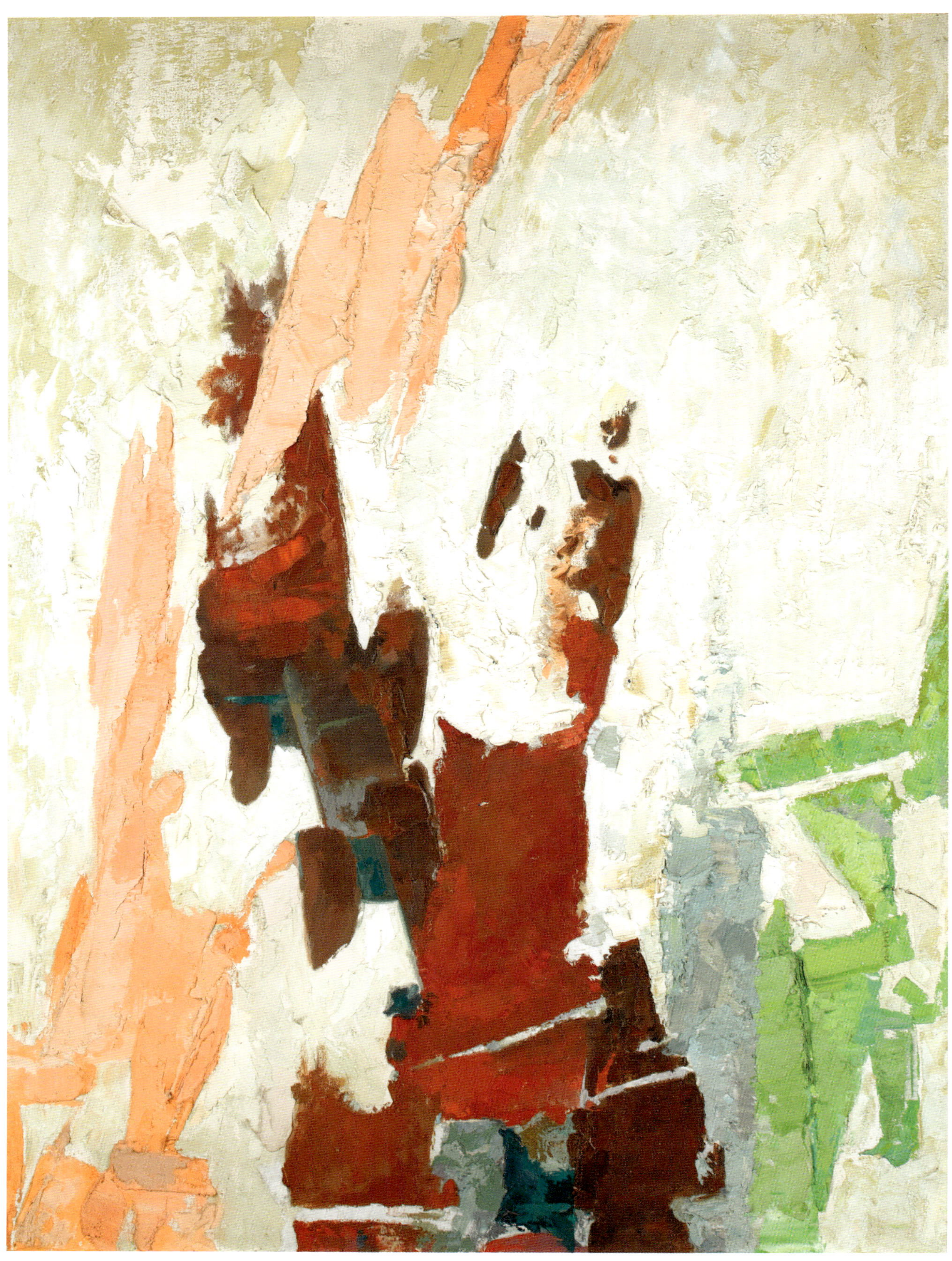

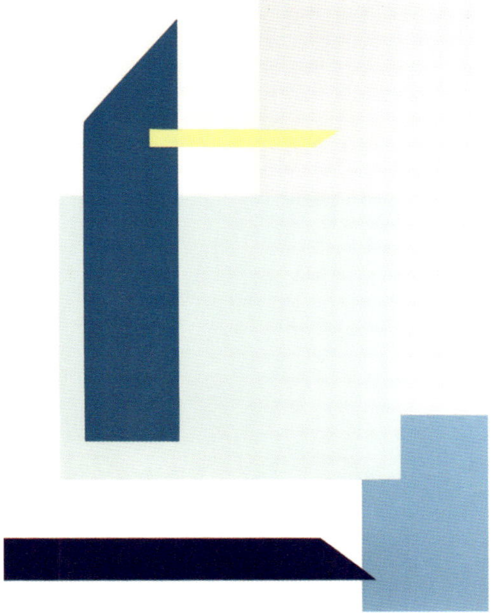

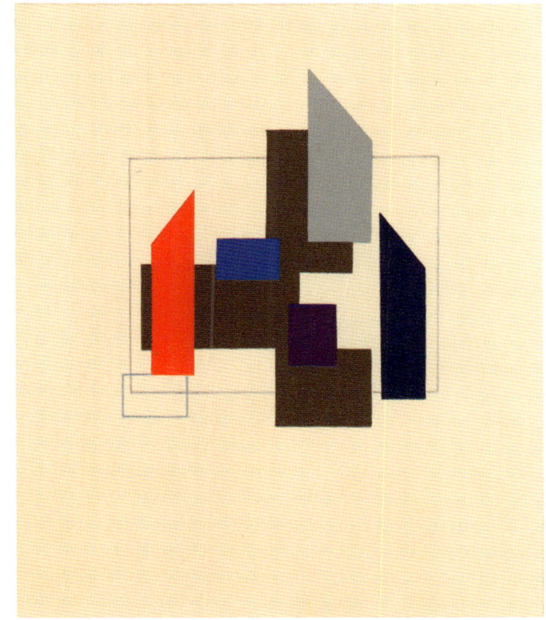

Fig. 3   Fig. 4

Kathleen Guthrie (1905-1981),

Fig. 3 – *Uprights*, from a tempera painting of 1936 by John Cecil Stephenson, mid 1960s, signed and inscribed, silkscreen print (edition of 14), 18 ½ × 14 ¼ in. (47 × 36 cm).

Fig. 4 – From a painting by Cecil Stephenson 1938, c 1960, signed and titled, silkscreen and crayon, 11 ¾ × 9 ¾ in. (30 × 25 cm).

from the continent, Stephenson was amongst the first artists in Britain to explore the new formal language of *Tachisme*, abandoning his former smooth tempera-like surfaces to produce brilliantly textured large scale canvases painted in impasto, each titled after a musical passage. (**Fig. 2**, **CAT. 31**, **34**) Read considered them amongst Stephenson's finest achievements: 'He created a world of visual delight that must at last be shared with a wide and appreciative public.'

Stephenson's first and only solo exhibition came late in his career – at the Drian Gallery – in 1960. In the foreword to the catalogue for this exhibition Read wrote: 'The vicissitudes of the art world are such that it is possible for an artist of great talent to work for a lifetime in obscurity, and only towards the end of his career find the recognition that is due to him . . . ' Tragically, in the same year of his Drian Gallery show, Stephenson suffered three strokes which left him unable to move or talk, bringing his momentous talent to a tragic standstill. A re-edition of three of Stephenson's pure abstracts from the 1930s as silkscreens, created by Stephenson's wife Kathleen Guthrie, offered a last flash of brilliance, (**Fig. 3**, **4**) but until his death in 1965 no further work was created.

Fig. 2 – *Cadenza 2*, 1959, signed, dated and titled on the reverse, oil on board, 48 × 36 in. (122 × 91.5 cm).
Provenance: Marjorie Guthrie.

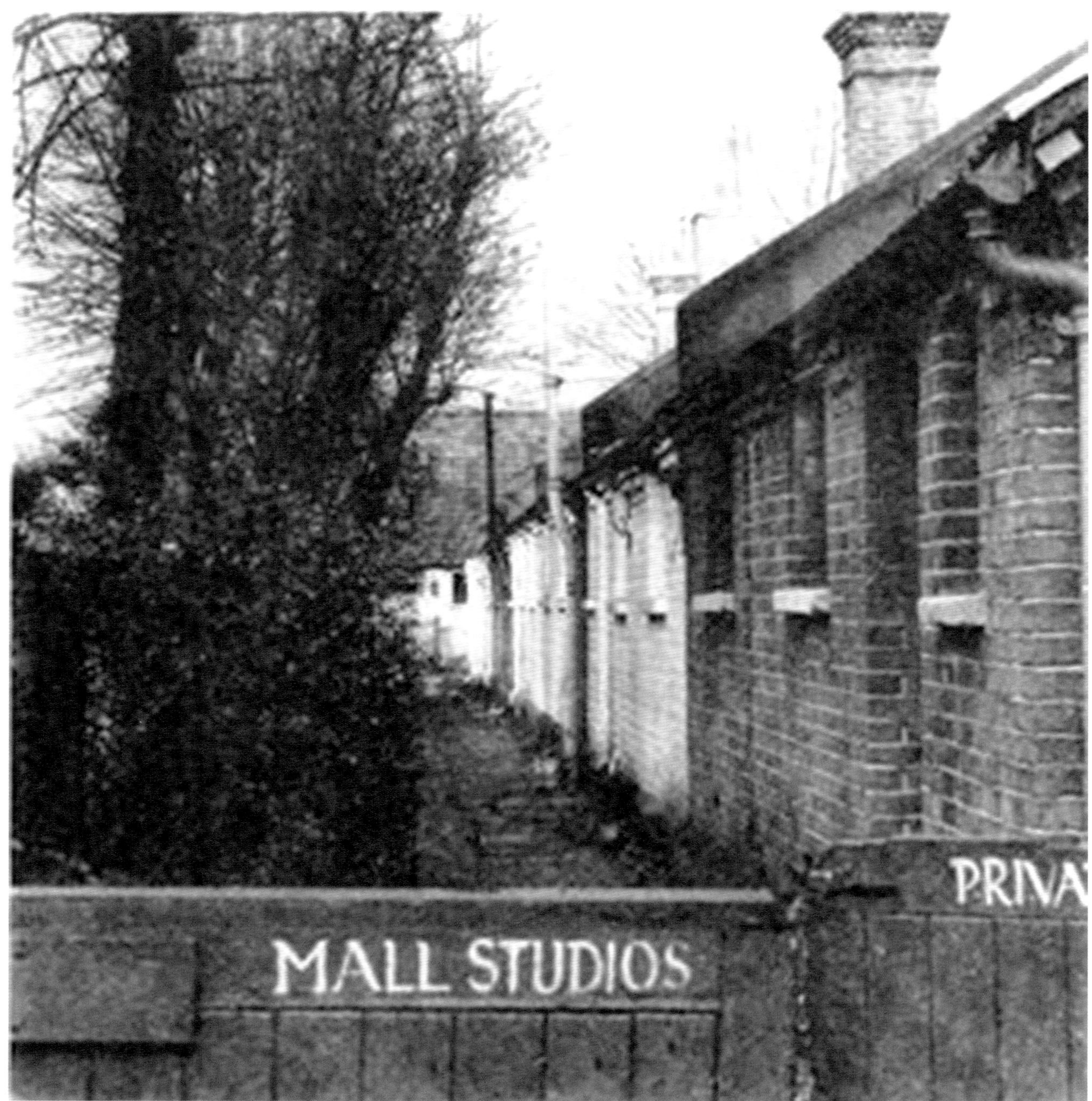

Fig. 5 – Mall Studios, c. 1930s.

Mall Studios, Hampstead

Michael Harrison

On 12th May 1937 Charles Ginner looked down from his first floor window at 61 Hampstead High Street. It was a view he had drawn and painted many times but, after all the cuffuffle of the abdication, this was the day of George VI's coronation and Flask Walk was festooned with blue and yellow pennants and the red, white and blue of Union Jacks. As usual, Ginner made a pencil and watercolour study, squared up, before transferring his composition to canvas. It was a method also used by Stanley Spencer who that August returned to the fair on the Heath and painted the helter-skelter.

A short walk away, Ben Nicholson, Naum Gabo and Leslie Martin were gathering together the essays for *Circle, an international survey of constructive art and architecture*, conceived as a counterblast to the great Surrealist exhibition of the previous year.

A year after its publication, Piet Mondrian (**Fig. 6**) would arrive as the final member of what Herbert Read labelled this 'nest of gentle artists' [1] – a 'saint in Hampstead' [2] as Barbara Hepworth recalled him, though for some he was all but the devil incarnate, and a protestant one at that, 'a Cubist shaved thin, a severe and tedious moralist', as the poet and critic Geoffrey Grigson insisted. [3]

* * *

With Sickert, Gilman, Gore and others, Ginner had been a member of the Fitzroy and Camden Town Groups but had moved up to Hampstead in 1919. Early that year a young north-eastern artist, returning to London after the disruption of the War, had met Sickert. He advised him to find a studio and, in March, John Cecil Stephenson installed himself at No. 6 The Mall, in Tasker Street off Parkhill Road. His thoughts were of developing a career as a portrait and landscape painter, unaware that he was the first of Herbert Read's nest.

Hampstead had long been a place for artists and writers, though not simply for their art. Constable had first gone there in 1819, one hundred years before Ginner and Stephenson, and eventually moved into Well Walk, where 'our little drawing room commands a view unequalled in Europe', [4] and where Keats had first found lodgings. The Constables' house looked down across an expanding but still separate London and in that first year they could well have met Keats and Coleridge walking on the Heath, talking about 'a thousand things'.[5] Keats had come to nurse his brother Tom, and Constable's move was in the hope of finding relief for his ailing wife. Tom and John Keats and Maria Constable would all soon die of tuberculosis, a disease which took its toll well into the 20th century when consumptives still escaped the London smog for the breezy heights of Hampstead. In 1918, on her doctor's recommendation, Katherine Mansfield took a house on East Heath Road with her new husband John Middleton Murry. Their on-off friend D.H. Lawrence had lived for a few months in 1915, nearby in the optimistically named Vale of Health, in between *The Rainbow* and *Women in Love*. Neither found a cure. Nor did the first wife of Geoffrey Grigson, living in the '30s in Keats Grove, the road rechristened after Keats' last and celebrated port-of-call in Hampstead.

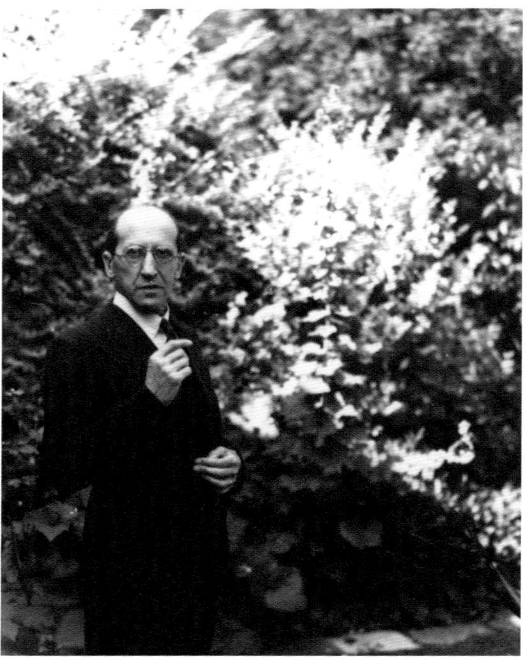

Fig. 6 — Piet Mondrian photographed by John Cecil Stephenson in the garden of 6 Mall Studios, 1939. (Estate of John Cecil Stephenson/Tate Archive).

A few doors down from Lawrence, but in better health, was the painter Henry Lamb. His studio, on the top floor of the Vale Hotel, now no longer there, overlooked the pond and would be taken over in 1923 by Stanley Spencer who, at that time, painted the roundabout in the fairground beneath the bedroom window. It may have been the roundabout which had inspired the *Merry-Go-Round* (**Fig. 7**) by Mark Gertler who had escaped the East End early in 1915, relishing the prospect of rural walks.

Spencer arrived at the Vale just as a young curator at the Tate Gallery moved into No. 1 Elm Row, up the hill from Ginner's flat, and round the corner from the Vale of Health. Jim Ede, who later created Kettle's Yard in Cambridge, began there what he came to call 'a way of life'. Living on a shoestring salary, he began to collect contemporary art and entertain artists, actors, writers, musicians and dancers with little food but on beautiful, old china and in rooms of poised simplicity. His great coup as a collector would be his acquisition — and rescue — of the estate of Henri Gaudier-Brzeska, who had been enthusiastically taken up and dropped by Mansfield and Murry before he went off to war.

By this time, of course, London and Hampstead were joined up, linked by the Northern Line and, from the 1840s, by the development of the Eton College-owned estate at Chalcots — hence Eton Avenue — and Belsize village becoming Belsize Park. Amid this burgeoning of fairly well-to-do and aspirational housing, *The Architect*, on 17th August 1872, announced 'works in hand' by Thomas Batterbury whose father had already been building what Andrew Saint has described as 'the rather weary houses of Parkhill Road' and who had spotted a potential market:

A range of eight studios, seven in a group, and one detached, are in course of erection on ground adjoining the garden priory of St. Dominic. Each studio is 25 feet by 20 feet and almost 20 feet to the ridge. . . . The light is from three skylights in each, in addition to a large window with a north-east aspect. The walls are of red bricks . . . . The cost of each studio will be £325 to £350. [6]

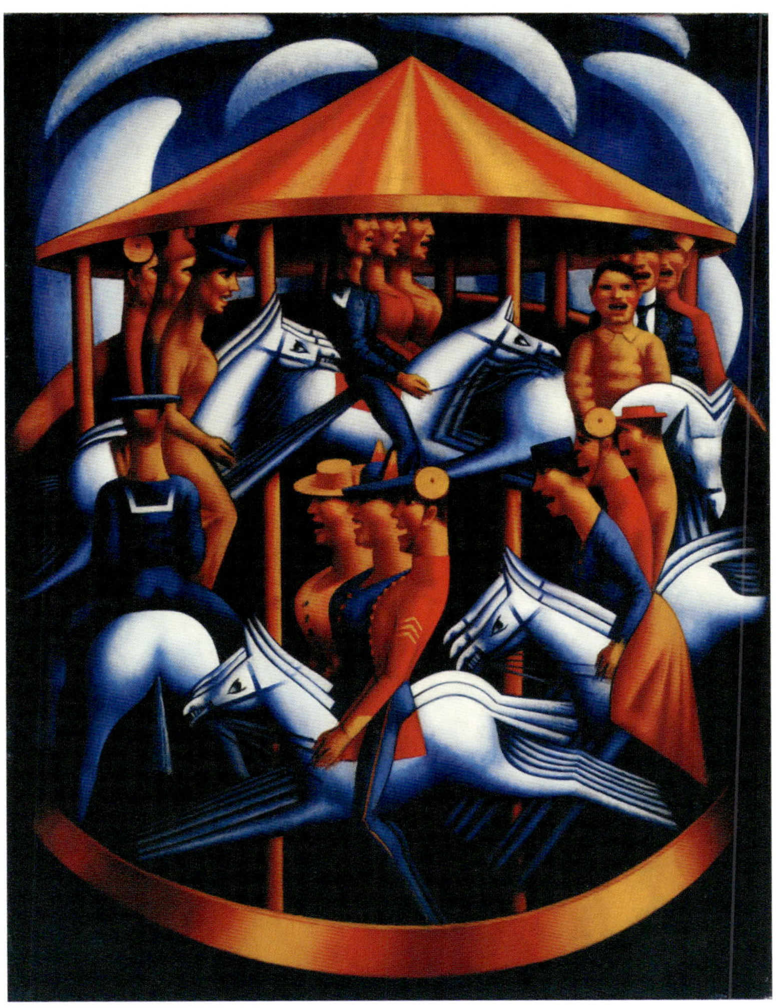

Fig. 7 – Mark Gertler (1891-1939), *Merry-Go-Round*, 1916,
oil on canvas, 74 ½ × 56 in. (189.2 × 142.2 cm). Collection: Tate Britain.

When Cecil Stephenson moved into his studio he was coming up to 30 but still something of an innocent abroad, single and sending his washing up north to his mother who also helped with money and the supply of furniture. He had been born in Bishop Auckland, County Durham in 1889 in fairly straitened circumstances. After a distinctly provincial art training in

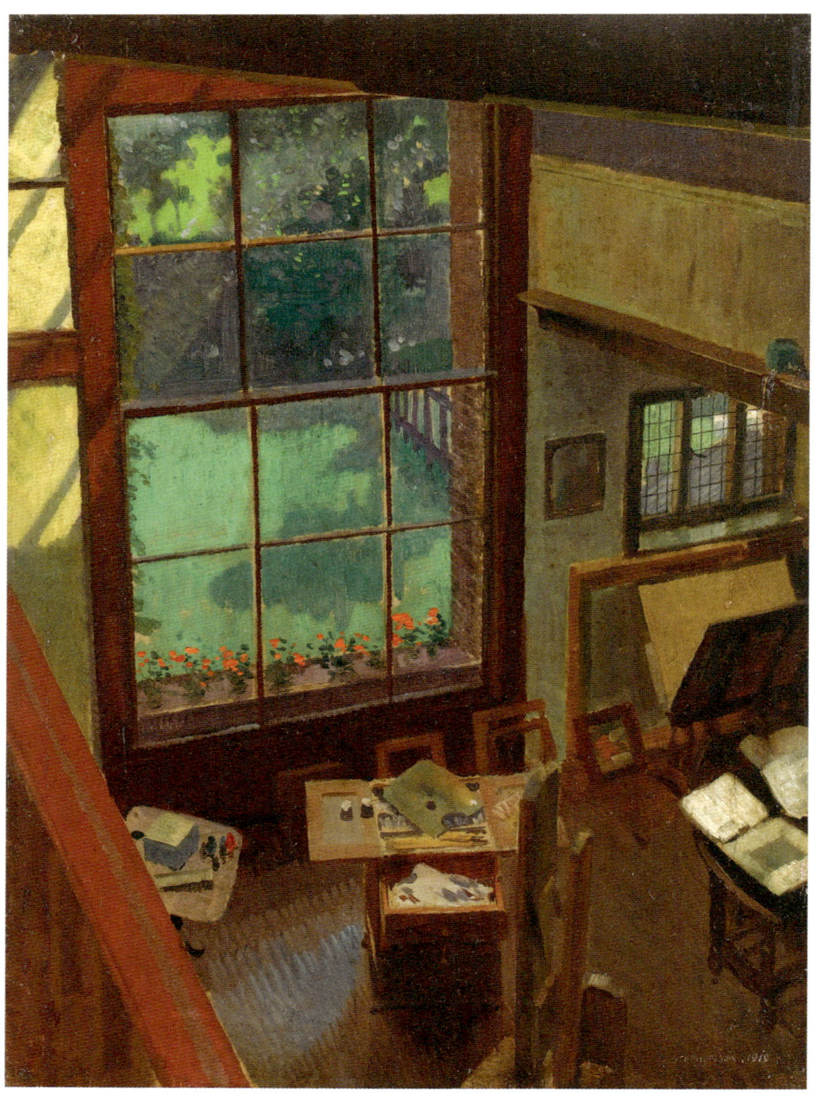

Cat. 2 – *The Artist's Studio, (Mall Studios, 6 Tasker Road, Hampstead)*, 1919, signed and dated with scratching out, signed in pencil on the reverse oil on panel, 16 x 11 ¾ inches. (40.5 x 30 cm). © The Artist's Estate

Darlington, he had transferred to Leeds School of Art where he stayed from 1909 until 1914, winning a silver medal for modelling a figure from the nude and being kept on as a pupil-teacher. As a Master of Sculpture and not convinced that a living was to be made from painting, he went on to the Royal College of Art to study silver- and goldsmithing. In September 1915 he moved over to the Slade, only to be called up for war service in December. Still in London, he was taught to make machine tools but by February he was back in Bishop Auckland, working in munitions at The Old Forge and grabbing what little time he could to ply his trade as a painter.

Returning to London, commissions were hard to come by and Stephenson continued to cultivate his northern clientele though this was insufficient. His brother urged him towards commercial design but in 1920 he took up a part-time teaching post at the Northern Polytechnic on Holloway Road and, remarkably, there he remained, promoted to Head of Art in the School of Architecture, Surveying and Building in 1922, until retirement in 1955.

And No. 6 The Mall was to be his home for the rest of his life. A painting, looking down into the studio from its balcony (**Cat. 2**), carries the excitement of new territory but would not have disturbed the hang of a Camden Town Group exhibition. He had read *Concerning the Spiritual in Art* as early as 1915 and in 1922 acquired and annotated his own copy, drawn to Kandinsky's analogies between the visual and the musical and the notion of 'expression without representation', but the path towards contemporary art was by no means clear. Friendship with two younger painters, Rodney Burn and Robin Guthrie, who adopted a derelict chapel in Parkhill Road as their studio and who shared their Slade Professor Henry Tonks' antagonism towards most things modern and foreign, which did little to encourage adventure. Nor did teaching at the Northern Polytechnic provide much in the way of artist contacts, though engagement with architects would be significant.

Life might have continued ever thus had new neighbours not moved into No. 7 around New Year 1928. The newcomers were Barbara Hepworth and her husband, John Skeaping, both recently back from the British School in Rome and soon to be exhibiting together at the Beaux Arts Gallery. Fourteen and twelve years their senior, a conventional painter off on a tour of northern castles and in the throes of building a large-scale model locomotive and railway in his garden, Stephenson must have seemed from another world and, apart from daily pleasantries, there was probably little exchange. Then, despite the arrival of their son Paul, the two young sculptors began to part ways and soon Hepworth was linking up with a very different artist who shared her ambition for a truly modern art.

The nest had already grown in 1929 to take in the newly married Henry Moore at 11a Parkhill Road (**Fig. 8**) but in 1931 Hepworth (**Fig. 9**) met Ben Nicholson and, by the end of the year, he had installed himself at No. 53. 1932 saw Stephenson married to Sybil Mason, intent on escape from Bishop Auckland; she and Barbara struck up a friendship and Cecil was soon building picture

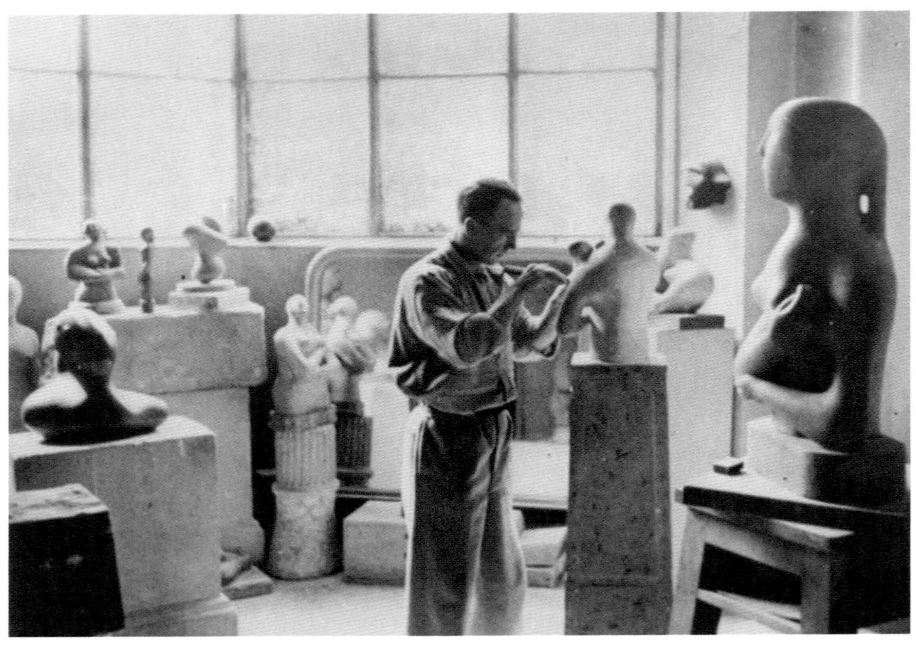

Fig. 8 – Henry Moore in his studio at 11a Parkhill Road, London in 1932.
© The Henry Moore Foundation. All Rights Reserved

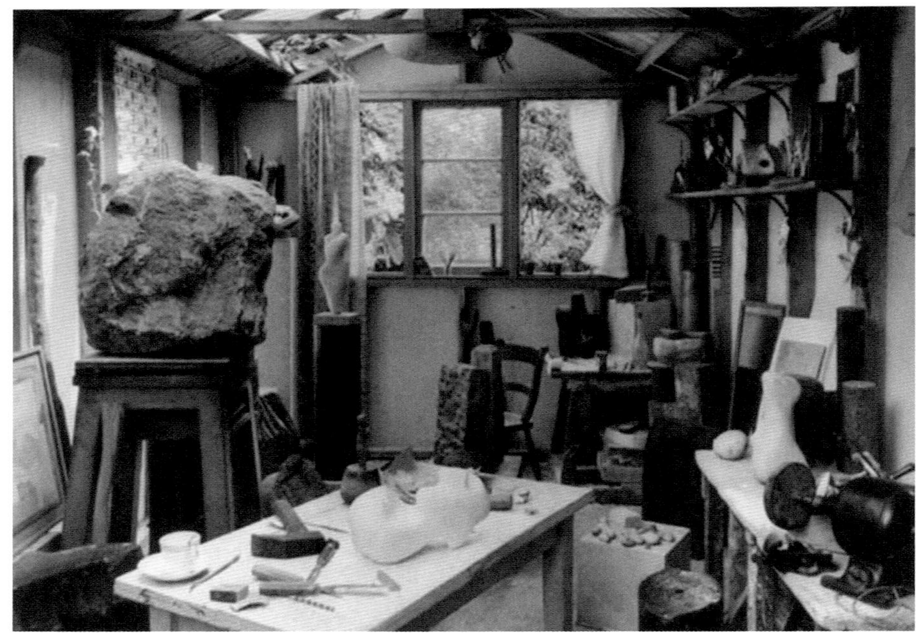

Fig. 9 – Barbara Hepworth's studio, The Mall, summer 1933.

racks for Ben. With Skeaping gone, Ben moved into The Mall and conversation picked up.

Ironically the rift in Ben Nicholson's marriage produced results. Winifred Nicholson decided to base herself in Paris and Ben paid frequent visits, ostensibly to visit the children, while both he and Barbara reaped the rewards of Winifred's new contacts with the artists of the *avant-garde*. He had long since felt the impact of Picasso without being able to put it to direct use. Now, with Barbara replacing Winifred as his immediate sounding board and Christopher Wood having died in 1930, his paintings were carrying shades of Braque and soon of Miró, while a visit to Arp's studio had a profound effect on Hepworth.

All this must have awoken Stephenson to new possibilities. He had read Kandinsky but seen next to nothing of his work, and English modernism was still in thrall to Roger Fry and Wyndham Lewis. With his creed of 'significant form' centred on Cézanne, Fry's Post-Impressionist exhibitions of 1910 and 1912 had been French in the first instance with a leavening of Russian and British second time round. But, as modern art unfolded in post-war years, he spied enemies in other camps. Miró and Masson, the 'two great Sure-realist painters' – Catalan and French – were somehow 'the revenge of Germany on France – ideography, symbolism, expressionism and all the possibilities of exploiting the public that these bring.' Paul Klee was a 'bloody German' with his 'fugal variations on cocks and cunts', and even the Pastoral Symphony showed 'the essential barbarity and want of civilisation of the German spirit.' [7] It was a tune to be taken up by Kenneth Clark who damned abstract art for its roots in German philosophy; 'We paid the price, as usual, the price for having conquered Germany materially by being in turn conquered by German culture.' [8] And it wasn't just Germany that had to be guarded against. 'France', Fry wrote to Virginia Woolf, 'is really the chief hope of any resistance to America.' [9]

Fry had earlier written to Vanessa Bell that

I'm getting an idea of what I think is the great thing in design, namely to have the greatest inter-play between the volumes and the spaces both at their three dimensionalest. . . . It means that both volumes and spaces function to the utmost against one another, as it were. [10]

The art historian and critic R.H. Wilenski was even more hard-line in his insistence on the formal aspects of art. For Wilenski all the artistic movements of the last hundred years had originated in Paris and the great event had been Cézanne 'turning his back on the Romantic heresy.' With a title like *The Modern Movement in Art*, it's not surprising that Stephenson should have grabbed it soon after publication in 1927. No doubt he responded to Wilenski's advocacy of a classical, 'architectural' approach to painting engendered by Cézanne and Seurat, with Picasso their anointed successor and Wyndham Lewis (**Fig. 10**) as the 'only English artist to see the point of Cubism pre 1914.' The truly modern artist had 'abandoned the emotive technique of the original romantics and the various degenerate forms of "free" emotive handling that derive from it.' [11]

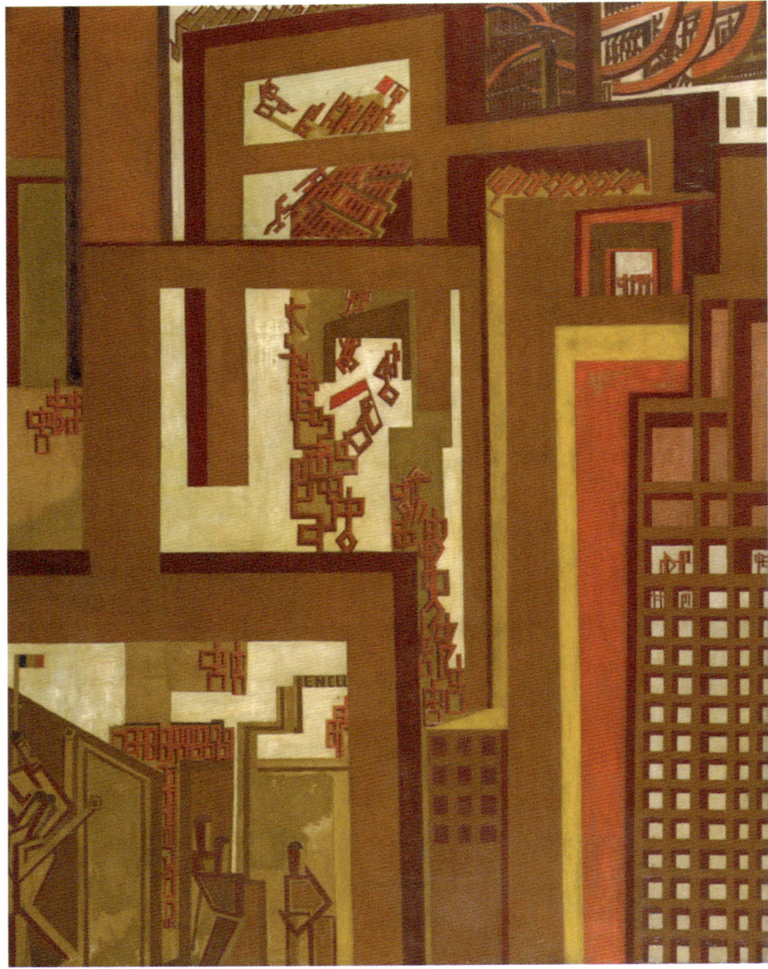

Fig. 10 – Wyndham Lewis (1882–1957), *The Crowd*, 1914-15,
oil and pencil on canvas, 79 × 60 ½ in. (200.7 × 153.7 cm). Collection: Tate.

***

Into the critical mix and into the nest came the very different voice of Herbert Read, anarchist, poet, art critic and one-time curator at the V&A, another Yorkshireman; he, Moore, Hepworth and Stephenson had all passed through Leeds. Read had made a false move in taking up a lectureship at Edinburgh University in 1931 and his discomfort was compounded by the social rejection which came with marital break-up and his relationship with a young professional viola player, Margaret 'Ludo' Ludwig. Returning to London in April 1933, they borrowed 11a Parkhill Road from Henry Moore and then moved into No.3 The Mall. Read was conscious that they had landed up in not the smartest part of town, 'on the frontier that divides the two worlds of Hampstead and Camden Town', [12] and Ludo was not too impressed: 'it was in rather a sort of more commonplace part of Hampstead.'[13] Their studio was soon regaled with Nicholson paintings and curtains and the famous red disc Ben set high on the chimney breast, but when Virginia Woolf came to dinner, she enquired of Read whether this was a stable, and, the following morning, wrote in her diary of

that vast comfortless studio, where none of the charm of Bohemia mitigated the hard chairs, the skimpy wine, & the very nice conversation. Henry Moore, sculptor & his Russian wife . . . Steel chairs, clear pale colours; talk of pots; brainy talk, specialists talk. Read devitalised: possibly his look – a shop assistant. [14] (**Fig. 11**)

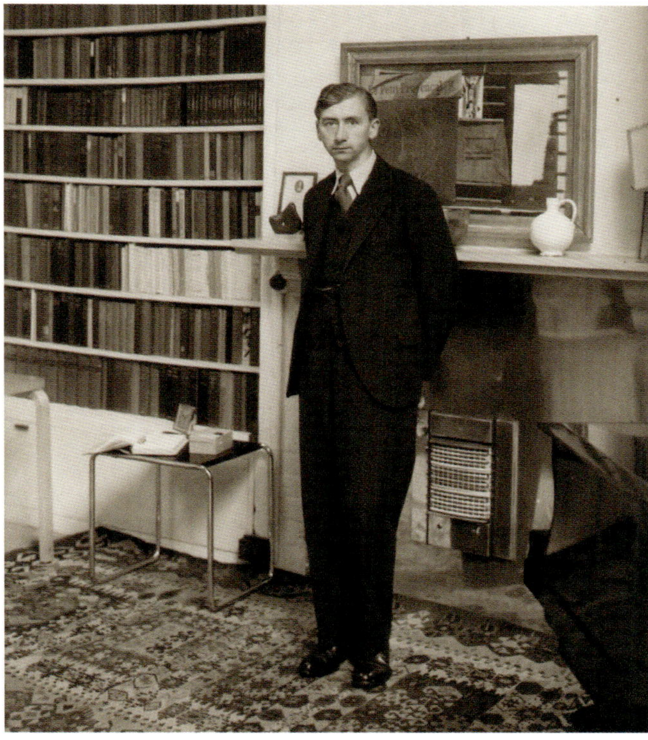

Fig. 11 – Herbert Read (1893-1968) in his home, No.3 The Mall, Parkhill Road, 1934, Photographed by by Howard Coster. © National Portrait Gallery, London.

For Ludo, a Catholic convert, it was not however without its compensations with St Dominic's next door:

There was a little passage, and if you went to the Priory and said one prayer, you nipped out at the other end and there you were in Kentish Town . . . and there was a movie there, just opposite the passage. You said a prayer, nipped out of church and into the movies.' [15]

And shopping was cheaper than on Haverstock Hill.

In 1933 Read had already published *The Meaning of Art*, and *Art Now* was about to appear. While, like Wilenski, he acknowledged the importance of Cézanne, his thinking about art had different roots. He claimed the German art historian Wilhelm Worringer, the author of Form and Gothic and Abstraction and Empathy, as 'my esteemed master' [16] and admitted a specifically northern trait of modern expressionism into a broader vision of modern art, beginning with Van Gogh and Munch, and leading on to 'that prolific German school, now so much in disfavour.' For Read

The greatest art includes both realism and romanticism, both the senses and the imagination. The greatest art is precisely this: a dialectic process which reconciles the contradictions derived from our senses on the one hand and our imagination on the other. [17]

In *Art Now*, he cited Gauguin as the discoverer of a new symbolic vision of the world and came to see Klee (**Fig. 12**) with his 'insistence, at one and the same time, on the subjective sources and the objective means of art' as 'the most significant artist of our epoch.' [18]

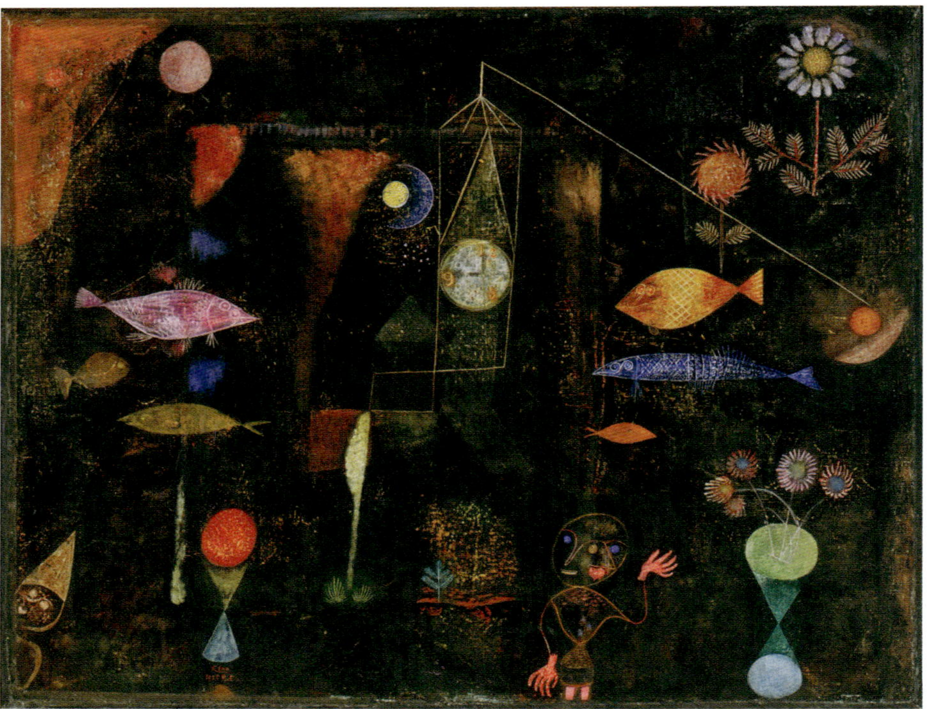

Fig. 12 – Paul Klee, (1879-1940) Fish Magic, 1925,
oil and watercolor on canvas on panel, 30 ½ × 38 ¾ in. (77.2 × 98.5 cm).
Collection: Philadelphia Museum of Art.

Whereas Cézanne sought reality through the shifting nature of perception of the external world,

the art of Klee is a metaphysical act. It demands a philosophy of appearance and reality. It denies the reality or sufficiency of normal perception; the vision of the eye is arbitrary and limited – it is directed outward. Inward is another and more marvellous world.' [19]

No wonder he got Roger Fry's back up who saw him as 'one of this neo-Thomist lot with a whole bag of metaphysical nostrums on his back' [20] though Fry succumbed to his appointment as editor of the *Burlington Magazine*, 'in spite of my distaste for his writings and his general *weltanschauung*.' [21] The job, at least, provided Read with one lifeline in a make-do economy, bolstered by a treadmill regime of reviewing.

Amongst English artists, Read's first instincts were towards the sculptor Henry Moore, for whom he wrote a career-launching monograph, published by Zwemmer in '34, and the painter Paul Nash. In 1932 Nash had let it be known that 'a marriage has been announced.' [22] The marriage was to be the formation of Unit One and was to be multi-dimensional. It gathered up artists and architects – Moore, Nash, Wadsworth, Hepworth, Nicholson, Burra, Armstrong, Hillier, Wells Coates et al – in an attempt to draw together and promote, with the help of Herbert Read, the conflicting strands of British surrealism and abstraction. An exhibition at the Mayor Gallery, under the direction of Douglas Cooper, was timed to co-incide with the launch of *Art Now* in October 1933. But unity among such a diverse group was short-lived and by the end of 1934 only Nash and Moore survived a unanimous vote.

The break-up was a signal that battle lines had been drawn. In April 1934 Nicholson paid Mondrian the first of several visits in Paris and emerged from his studio bewitched but self-confessedly bemused, captivated by the hanging panels of colour and the entire experience, convinced of the import of the paintings, though unable to grasp quite what they were doing. Of one thing he was certain and, as chairman of the Seven and Five society of painters and sculptors, he returned to decree that henceforth only non-figurative work would be exhibited. Though not a member, Cecil Stephenson had attended that and at least one earlier meeting but it was his luck that he started to exhibit with a prestigious society that was about to crumble under the weight of its new regulation. The Leicester Galleries refused an all-abstract show and the exhibition at Zwemmer's Gallery in October 1935 turned out to be a flop.

***

Meanwhile foundations of modernity had literally been laid two streets up from Parkhill Road. In 1929 Jack Pritchard, Hampstead born and bred, an 'entrepreneur' by his own account, and his wife Molly had joined up with the Canadian Wells Coates, an engineer by training, to form a design company which soon became Isokon Ltd. Now, in 1933, the

Pritchards asked Wells Coates to design a building of new flats in Lawn Road. Pritchard and Coates, together with Serge Chermayeff, had visited the Bauhaus at Dessau in 1931 and Coates had been deeply impressed by the workers' flats designed by Gropius. With first-hand experience both of the bleakness of London bedsit-land and the economy of Japanese house design – and with strong views about notions of property – he was interested in designing spaces for the needs of modern living. Molly Pritchard's draft prospectus spoke of

ready-to-live-in flats . . . designed for business men and women who have no time for domestic troubles. Everything unnecessary, ugly, inconvenient and 'labour-making' has been eliminated and yet everything essential is there, and is there in exactly the right position.

The Isokon Flats (**Fig. 13**) boasted beds and tables that folded up, maid service, laundry collection and a communal kitchen, soon to be remodelled as the Isobar restaurant.

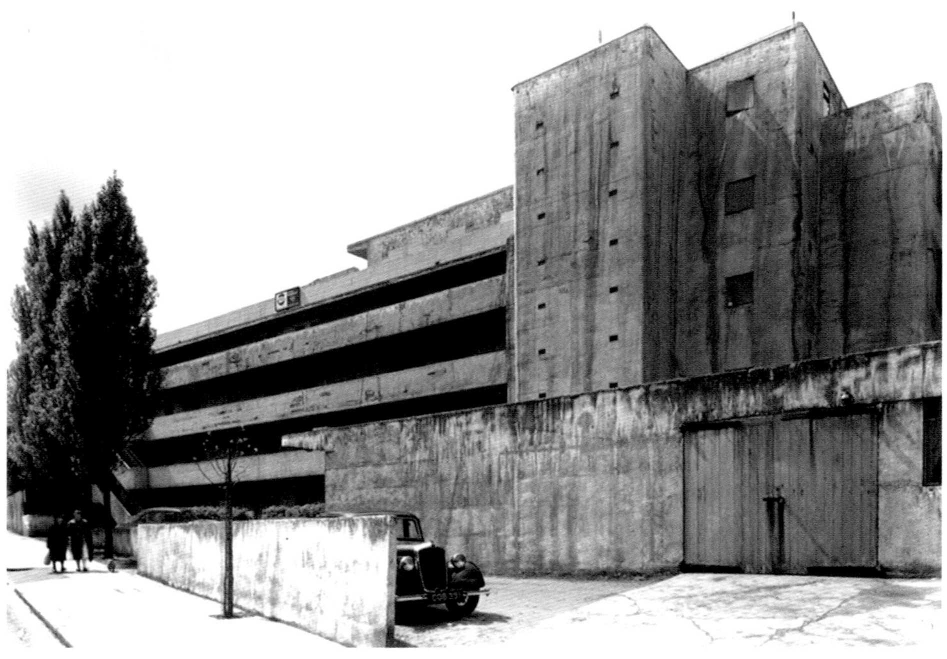

Fig. 13 – Designed by Wells Coates for Jack and Molly Pritchard, the Isokon Building opened in 1934 as a progressive experiment in new ways of urban living. It was the first block ever to be built chiefly using reinforced concrete. It was painted brown to avoid being bombed during the war.

Though remarkably modest and understated, their impact must have been extraordinary, not least the rounded zigzag staircase linking the walkways which serve each floor; this in contrast to their nearby Victorian counterparts, each house with its hefty and portentous front steps leading to its *piano nobile*. The flats were not alone as new building in the area but steel-framed windows and Art Deco canopies do not break the pattern of the latterday Arts and Crafts houses across the road. Voted the second most ugly building in England by Cyril Connelly's readers in Horizon in 1946, this 'huge and lovely Atlantic liner' was a source of wonder to Ben Nicholson and, no doubt, to others living in The Mall. Sybil Stephenson had already bought Isokon furniture to replace Cecil's mother's Victorian hand-me-downs and painted what couldn't be replaced with white emulsion. And Cecil himself was not immune, acquiring copies of Bauhaus *Bucher No.14* at some time in the early '30s.

In his preface to *Art Now*, Herbert Read set the development of 20th century art in an alarming political climate with the Nazis having come to power in Germany. Within weeks of its opening in 1934, with the Pritchards taking the penthouse flat, the Isokon building unexpectedly began to play host to those from the Bauhaus — now refugees — who had inspired it. On 18th October Jack Pritchard, together with Morton Shand and Maxwell Fry, co-founders with Wells Coates of the MARS group, welcomed Walter Gropius, complete with new wife, at Victoria Station. Lodging first in Wildwood Terrace, off the north of the Heath, they quickly took up residence in Lawn Road and Fry offered him a partnership. The next year Marcel Breuer and Moholy-Nagy followed, Breuer succeeding Gropius in Isokon furniture design and designing the Isobar.

***

With Fascism in Europe, depression and unemployment at home, artists in England were facing questions about their practice in relation to their times as never before. Roger Fry died in 1934 and Herbert Read observed:

Faced with the machine, mass production, and universal education, [he] could only retreat into the private world of his own sensibility. [23]

But some of Fry's successors were more engaged. *Art Now* was followed by Read's *Art and Industry* in 1935, with *Art and Society* to come two years later, and Barbara Hepworth, as her patron and guardian angel Margaret Gardiner recalled, 'with her Yorkshire background and early memories of miners and mill-hands, was always concerned with politics and social problems.' [24] She, Nicholson and Paul Nash exhibited in 'Artists against Fascism and War' in 1935, organised by the newly formed Artists' International Association, and her thinking about art in its broader context was galvanised by the arrival in Spring 1936 of another *immigré*, the Russian Constructivist Naum Gabo (**Fig. 14**). Hepworth and Nicholson had met Gabo in Paris and encouraged him to come to London, and they brought him to Herbert Read's studio where he also met Cecil Stephenson. No. 3 The Mall had, by now, become well known as a meeting place and a place of parties, of a different character to those of Jim Ede up at Elm Row, though Hepworth and Nicholson frequented them both. As Geoffrey Grigson recounted of Read's studio:

It was where nationalities and generations mixed . . . Braque might be there, or Jean Hélion, from Paris, or Eliot gayer than his reputation, actually singing 'Frankie and Johnnie'. [25]

Gabo quickly felt more at home in what Hélion called 'the English Bateau Lavoir' than he had in Paris:

The mere presence of Herbert Read at that time meant that we could meet and talk within the terms of a philosophy. . . . He was more like a magnet which brings together people and ideas. . . . Herbert Read made England that central point from which our ideas spread. [26]

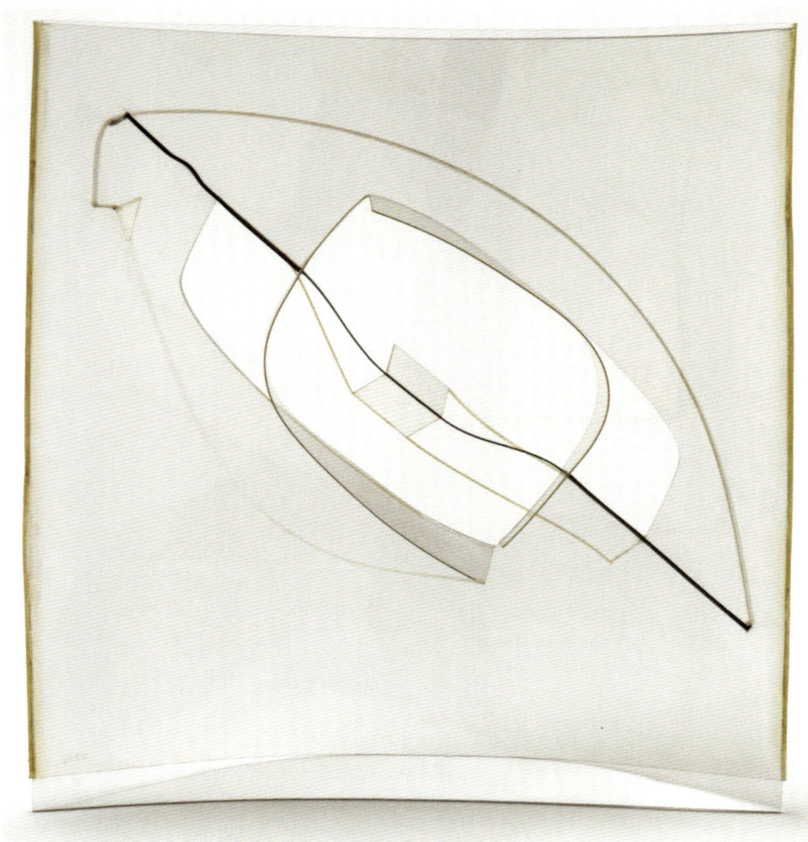

Fig. 14 – Naom Gabo (1890-1977), *Construction on a Line*, 1937,
Perspex, 17 ¾ × 17 × 3 ½ in. (45 × 43 × 9 cm). Collection: Tate.

The conversations were expansive. Gabo and Hepworth, in particular, shared a passionate interest in the relationship of art and science and their discussions were joined by Margaret Gardiner's partner the crystallographer J.D. Bernal. Gabo offered a positive vision of the 'constructive idea' as the counter to the destructive explosion of cubism and the challenge which had come with the theory of relativity.

Hepworth was conscious of her position as a sculptor chipping away at stone in her studio. (**Fig. 15**) She feared 'the cold power of the machine age' and that:

the speed is out of proportion in the world of invention to the detriment of poetry and aesthetic vision . . . I cannot see any hope of stopping this suicidal impulse unless Art & Science stand firm together.[27]

but she thought there would be 'a new form of ethics – social and political – very much to the good & what we had hoped for.'

I think the only way in which people of our generation will go on making a useful contribution is to accept the fact that certain privileges such as leisure, continuity, exclusive privacy, quietness & a host of other things are gone for ever. . . .We are much preoccupied (all of us) in thoroughly working out the living status of artist to society & that will never be solved by a commission of Fine Arts but only by the artist being allowed to take his place along with other workers.[28]

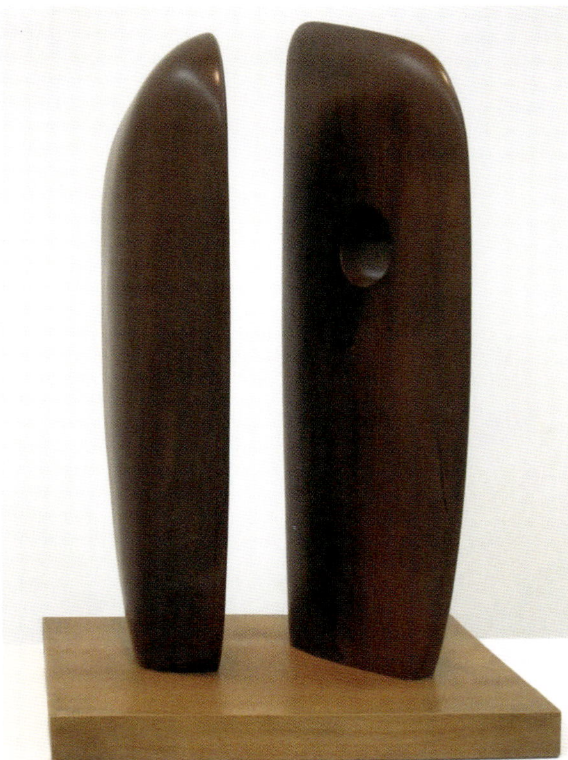

Fig. 15 – Barbara Hepworth (1903–1975),
Forms in Echelon, 1938,
Tulipwood on elm base
42 ½ × 23 ½ × 28 in. (108 × 60 × 71 cm).
Collection: Tate.

Their arguments would soon be gathered up for publication but before that an intrusion was brewing; 'An intrusion it was, an invasion from Paris which took place in 1936.' [29] For Roland Penrose, aghast at the snobbishness of England in comparison to France where he had been living, was determined, with the young poet David Gascoyne, to bring Surrealism to London. Paul Nash, Henry Moore and Herbert Read were recruited to the cause. There was also a French committee including Breton, Eluard and Man Ray. The result was the International Surrealist Exhibition, held at the New Burlington Galleries in June-July 1936 though contrived in Hampstead, with Penrose coming to live in Downshire Hill, up the road from Margaret Gardiner, and Paul Nash across Rosslyn Hill in Eldon Grove. (**Fig. 16**)

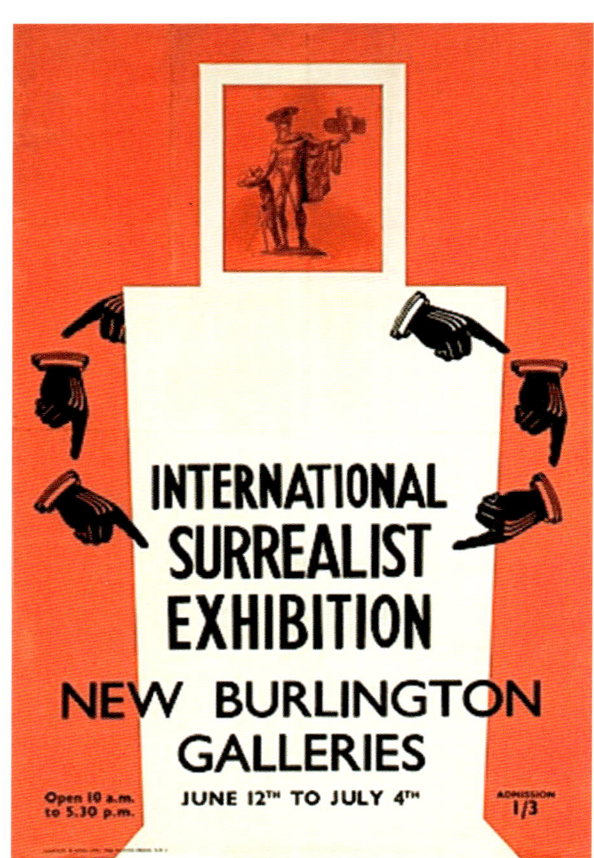

Fig. 16 – Poster for the first International Surrealist Exhibition held at the Burlington Galleries in 1936. Max Ernst contributed the modified image of the *Apollo Belvedere*.

Herbert Read confessed to being 'in the position of a circus rider with his feet placed astride two horses,' but saw nothing incompatible in supporting both abstract and surrealist camps. For him, one balanced the other: the abstract and constructive proceeding 'on the basis of the abstract concepts of physics and dynamics, geometry and mathematics', surrealism proceeding on 'the assumption of, the knowledge embodied in psycho-analysis.' [30] He championed Nicholson and Gabo but his personal preference was for organic rather than geometric abstraction and so for artists such as Moore and Arp who identified themselves with surrealism. Steeped in Freud but increasingly drawn to Jung, he saw surrealism, in this country, as a natural extension of the tradition of William Blake, Edward Lear and Lewis Carroll.

Another writer, soon to become a painter, would have none of it. Adrian Stokes, an early occupant of the Lawn Road flats, had written articles in the *Spectator* in 1934 about Moore, Hepworth and Nicholson. Now he was writing his sequel to *The Stones of Rimini*, for which Nicholson had designed the dust-jacket, applying its plea for 'a carving conception' to painting, and lamenting how 'few artists find their religion in the world of space.' Having been in analysis with Melanie Klein since 1930, in *Colour and Form*, he lambasted 'Surrealists who attempt (in vain) to reproduce the material of the unconscious in the raw':

the ignorant, half-baked and journalese theory of Surrealism. No one with first-hand experience of psycho-analysis — that is to say with first-hand knowledge of his own unconscious and its method of manifestation — has paid, or will pay, attention to the theory of Surrealism, except to view it as a symptom. [31] '

Nothing is more contrary to the essential esthetic faculty than the dream,' Roger Fry had told an audience of psycho-analysts, invoking Mallarmé. By contrast, painting based on formal relations, 'detached from the instinctive life', put artists on equal terms with scientists, though, he acknowledged, 'constantly in conflict with the mass of mankind which is deeply concerned with life and completely indifferent to truth.' [32]

In 1938 Sigmund Freud would come to live in Hampstead, first in Elsworthy Road and finally Maresfield Gardens.

***

Ben Nicholson, Barbara Hepworth and Naum Gabo went together to see the Surrealist exhibition and dived into an ABC tea shop afterwards to recover and plot the constructivist response. Drawing in the young architect, Leslie Martin, they planned an international anthology advocating 'a unity of social and cultural purpose pervading the whole of life.' 'We must re-establish first,' wrote the architectural critic J.M. Richards, 'that unity of purpose — that settled continuity of social life and of the formal expression of it.' [33]

For the contributors to *Circle*, human functions had become separated with the machine age: art from science, architecture from structure, creativity from making, artist from public. 'The romantic outlook [had seen] the machine essentially as a creator of ugliness — a dehu-manising agent.' 'Popular taste, caste prejudice, and the dependence upon private enterprise [had come] completely [to] handicap the development of new ideas in art.' [34] The 19th century had brought celebrity architects, indulging themselves in capricious variations of style while engineers, like Paxton and Brunel, had produced the real architecture. Martin pointed to 'the fact that the general public does not as yet observe the incongruity between its motor cars and its tudor villas,' and Hepworth objected that 'the form consciousness of people has become atrophied.'

Hepworth may have feared the 'cold power of the machine age' but *Circle* was not an occasion for sentimental retreat into medievalism such as Eric Gill's lament: 'since industrialism overwhelmed us … only in the fine arts do we preserve the notion that art is *man's* work.' [35] Denial left the machine unmastered and now was the time for its potential to be harnessed to the needs of society with a new awakening of the arts. There was no place for fantasy but the intuitive self needed to be rediscovered, ideas being born 'through a perfect balance of our conscious and unconscious life.' [36] Bernal saw how art could inform science: 'the artist has been busy solving problems in practice for which the theoretical formulation is yet largely wanted.' Maxwell Fry looked to 'the possible harmony existing between industrialisation and human welfare' in place of the speculative building that had come to dictate our urban environment and 'the well-worn paths of the Garden City movement and the C.P.R.E.' Planning was of the essence – this as Berthold Lubetkin's Health Centre was under construction across in the 'people's republic' of Finsbury. Up in Keats Grove, Geoffrey Grigson decried abstract art which promoted collectivity and socialism.

***

Circle, published by Faber & Faber, London in 1937, included an illustration of Cecil Stephenson's *Dynastatic* (**Fig. 17**) and that year saw him at his most prolific and most confident as an abstract painter. Gradually the self-conscious north-easterner had established his place in the Hampstead nest. His move towards abstract painting had come via figurative paintings of the machines which inhabited his studio. For him there was no fear of the machine and his engineering expertise brought a rapport with Naum Gabo and particularly with Alexander Calder when he came to stay in Hampstead for five months that year. Stephenson was at the party thrown by Hepworth and Nicholson to welcome Léger and Calder and then threw his own and, in December played host to a performance of Calder's *Circus*. With Nicholson he shared an enthusiasm for cars and, while Nicholson and Stokes played tennis, Stephenson honed his diving skills and taught Miriam Gabo to swim. Equally, he was at home with architects and came to know Wells Coates, Lubetkin, and Maxwell Fry, while also pursuing scientific interests through microscope and telescope. But there remained the sense of him as the handy neighbour, ever available to mend a clock; when Jim Ede needed his Brancusi *Golden Fish* fixing, he would turn to Stephenson for help and, when Nicholson and Hepworth were at last free to marry, Stephenson made the rings and stood as witness. Gabo later regretted him being 'badly neglected'. [37]

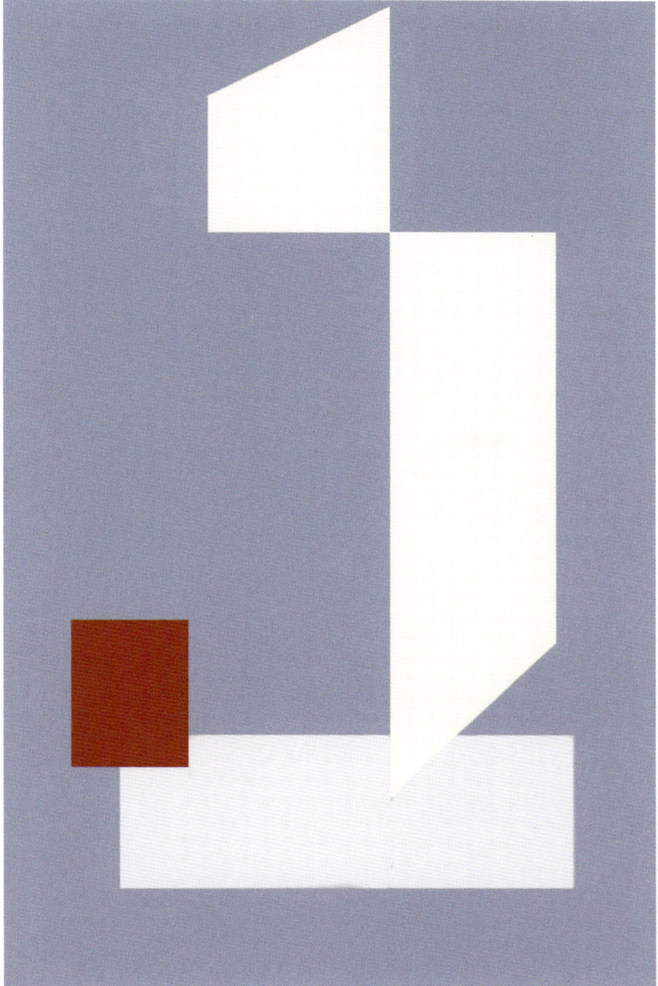

Fig. 17 – John Cecil Stepehnson (1889-1965)
Dynastatic, 1937
tempera on canvas laid on board,
48 x 30 inches (122 x 76 cm).
Courtesy of Jonathan Clark Fine Art
Private Collection.
© The Artist's Estate.

***

On the face of it, *Circle* marked the high point of abstract and constructive art in this country but the cracks were all too apparent. The Bauhaus had gone in 1933 and, in Paris, Abstraction-Création had begun to founder in 1934, only months after Hepworth and Nicholson had joined. The market in Europe for abstract work, such as it had ever been, declined, galleries closed or shifted their allegiances, and artists were looking to England for some glimmer of hope. John Piper had followed Ben Nicholson to Mondrian's door and joined him at the Seven and Five in his campaign for abstract art. Now his wife-to-be, Myfanwy Evans, was persuaded by Jean Hélion to launch a magazine to spread the abstract word – 'if not we shall starve and become either as dry as paper or green with mould.' [38]

AXIS, 'a quarterly review of contemporary "abstract" painting & sculpture' — the quotes were dropped in Autumn '36 — ran to eight issues, from January 1935 to early winter 1937. *AXIS 1* (**Fig. 18**) was notable for the first UK illustration of a Mondrian painting; the first edition of Herbert Read's *Art Now* had not included him. But the gainsayers were there from the outset, Geoffrey Grigson distinguishing between two kinds of abstraction, biomorphic on the one hand and geometric on the other, the latter 'abstractions which lead to the inevitable death.' Even Hélion, in *AXIS 2*, saw pure abstraction as suffering from an 'extreme limitation'. *AXIS 5* in Spring 1936 was devoted to Nicolete Gray's valiant touring exhibition 'Abstract & Concrete', but by *AXIS 6* Evans was noting that artists, Hélion and Piper among them, reserved 'the right to alter according to their own inclination and nature, and not according to a group programme.' Come the Autumn issue, Piper had reneged:

Any Constable, any Blake, any Turner — (and it was characteristic that he focussed on English artists) — has something an abstract or a surrealist painting cannot have. . . . The point is fullness and completeness; the abstract qualities of all good painting together with the symbolism (at least) of life itself. Today, both cannot go together.

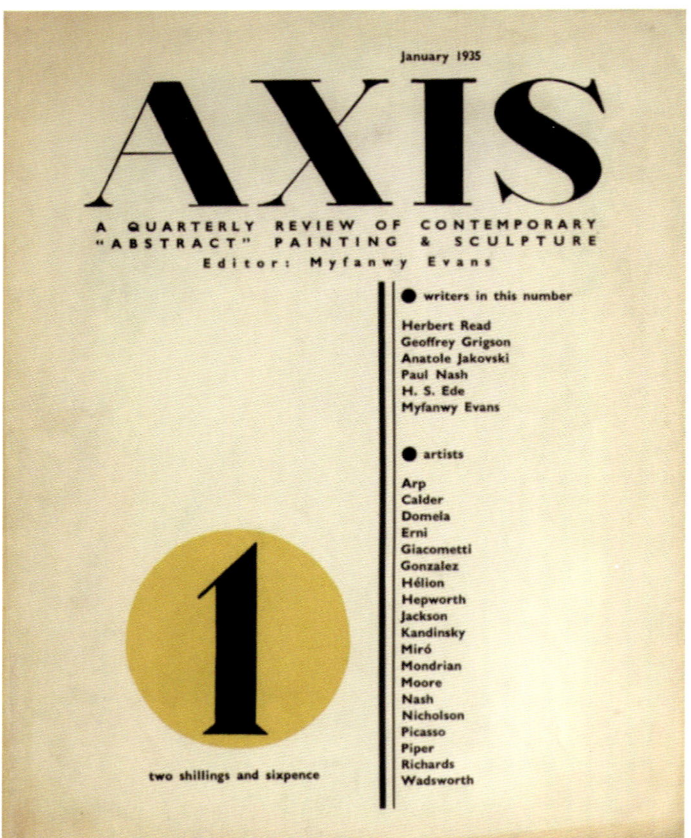

Fig. 18 – *AXIS*, January 1935 issue, a quarterly review of contemporary abstract painting & sculpture.

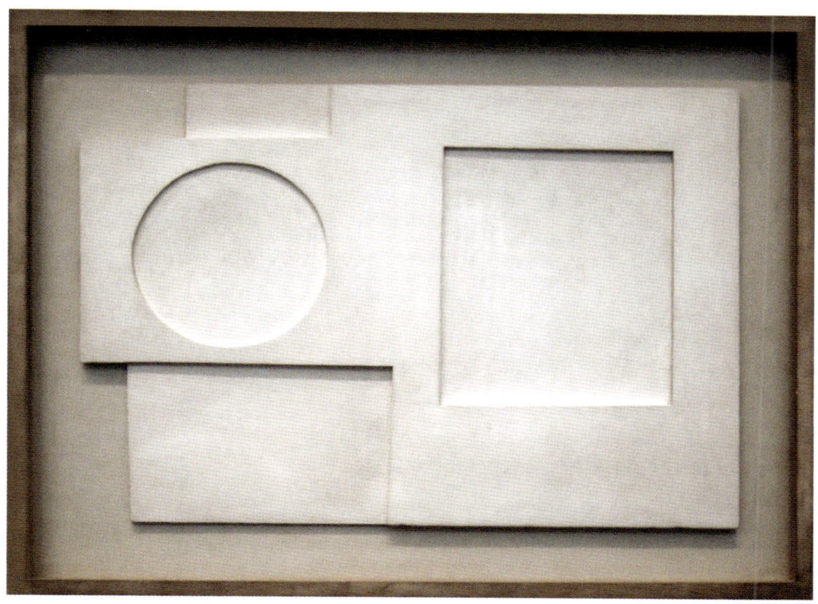

Fig. 19 — Ben Nicholson (1894–1982), *1934 (relief)*, 1934,
oil paint on mahogany, 71.8 × 96.5 × 3.2 cm). Collection: Tate.

It was all reminiscent of the argument conducted in the Listener, in Autumn 1935, between Kenneth Clark and Herbert Read, in which Clark had renewed Roger Fry's diatribe against all things German. Clark dismissed 'abstract art, in anything like a pure form' as having 'the fatal defect of purity' and, while he had condescended to buy a white relief from Ben Nicholson, he remarked 'many of us who enjoy Mr. Nicholson's paintings do so, I am afraid, less as cosmic symbols than as tasteful pieces of decoration.' [39] (**Fig 19**) 'Looking back,' he later wrote in his memoir,

I wonder how much I was ever persuaded by the doctrine of 'pure form'. If I had been asked for an honest answer, I suppose I would have admitted that subject-matter, with all its implications, was overwhelmingly important to me. And so perhaps would Roger, as his earlier and later writings show. [40]

By 1938 John Piper was exhibiting collages of English seaside towns alongside abstract paintings, no doubt in the hope of a more lucrative market.

***

The coronation had passed, the Spanish Civil War raged and the situation in Germany became more threatening by the week. Penrose brought *Guernica* to London. A largely taciturn Henry Moore, who had joined the Communist Party, sat on the Committee of

F.I.L. – 'For International Liberty' – with Margaret Gardiner as Secretary. Also in Downshire Hill, in the house where Stanley Spencer had courted Hilda Carline, the painter and writer Fred Uhlman, himself a German Jewish refugee, and his wife Diana operated the Artists' Refugee Committee, helping a steady flow of European exiles and eventually putting up John Heartfield for several years. The distinctly left-wing Free German League of Culture had its base in Upper Park Road after its first meetings at the Uhlmans.

For Mondrian the move to London was not simply a matter of fleeing Fascism but one of economic necessity and a need for companionship. Almost all his recent sales had been to English customers via the Nicholsons and perhaps there was a market to be cultivated. Ironically, Mondrian had excused himself from the exhibition which went with Circle, distressed by the hard-line exclusion of the Arps, Jean Gorin and Marlow Moss, his first English disciple.

He came on 21st September 1938, accompanied by Winifred Nicholson, and, after a few days in a nearby hotel, moved into a room at the back of No. 60 Parkhill Road, looking onto Ben Nicholson's studio in The Mall. Friends scurried to help with bedding and wondered at his adaptation of orange boxes and his detachment from material needs. Something of the magic of his Paris studio, with its red, blue and yellow panels, was recreated but, unsettled as he was, particularly after the fall of Paris, his two years in London were not especially productive. *Snow White* at the Odeon and dance halls across the frontier in Camden Town provided some distraction but his demoralisation would appear complete with Gabo brow-beating him into relinquishing the tag of 'neo-plasticist' and succumbing to 'constructivist'. [41]

He had arrived as the nest had all but dispersed. The Edes had left for Tangiers in 1936. Gropius, Breuer and Moholy headed to the USA the following year. Late in 1937 Read himself had retired to Beaconsfield where, as he wrote to Douglas Cooper, 'I shall have a dachshund & grow roses & forget about communism and surrealism.' [42] Adrian Stokes had moved out of Lawn Road and installed himself in Fitzroy Street, Sickert's old territory, two doors along from what became the Euston Road School where he developed his 'world of space' in still life painting. With war approaching, he and Margaret Mellis moved down to Cornwall and, within days of its outbreak, Nicholson and Hepworth packed the triplets into a hastily acquired old car and joined them in Carbis Bay, Ben re-engaging with still life and landscape and painting the view from the window. The Gabos followed on but Mondrian declined.

When war was declared only Mondrian, Stephenson and Moore, who took on No. 7 The Mall, remained. The death of Stephenson's painter friend, Jessica Dismorr, must have added to the sense of desolation. Stephenson and Mondrian clearly had an empathy for each other, each in their way outsiders, each with their own modesty, but Stephenson now as an exhibiting colleague, no longer in the shadow of more ambitious and class con-scious friends. Mondrian was on his own, Stephenson cuckolded by a Surrealist rival, E.L.T.

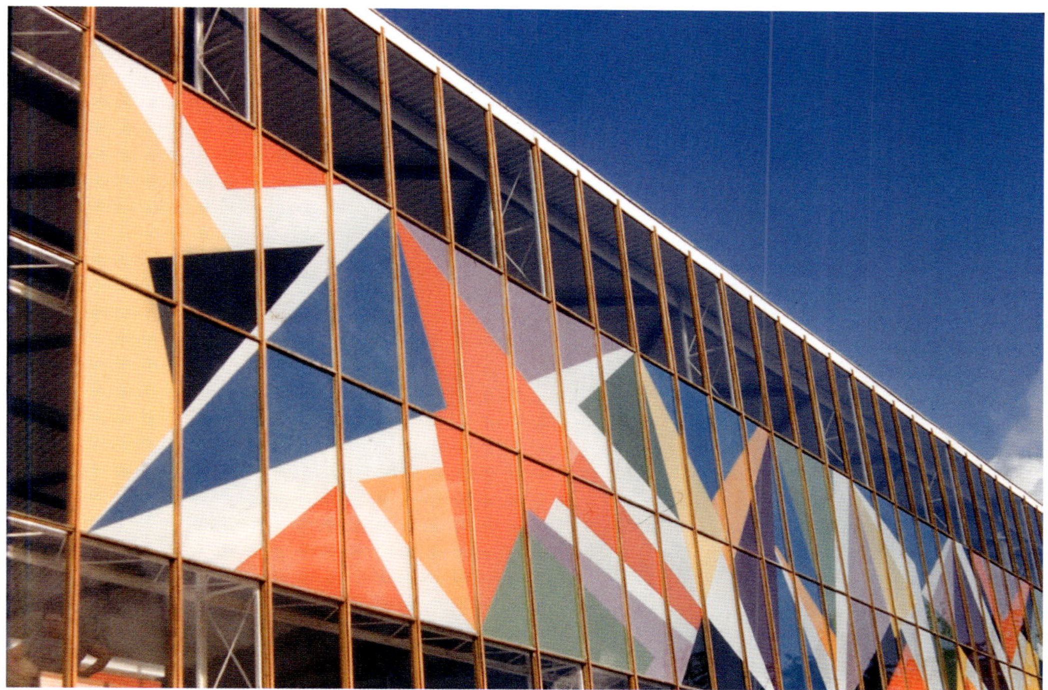

Mesens who ran the London Gallery, though Sybil was soon replaced by Kathleen Guthrie, separated from her husband Robin. With the phoney war over, the almost immediate bombing of Parkhill Road, exactly opposite Mondrian's house in September 1940, saw him swiftly onto a boat for New York and Moore retreated to Perry Green.

Hampstead was over but Stephenson stayed. There were paintings of the bombings and figure pictures to make ends meet but at core he remained true to his abstract vision. The Festival of Britain brought a commission for a large abstract ceiling painting and architectural projects followed in the '50s. (**Fig 20**) He would preside at Hampstead Artists' Council meetings and recognition followed with purchase by the Arts Council, a first one-man exhibition, introduced by Herbert Read, and eventual acquisition by the Tate, though not before a stroke had ended his career life as an artist.

The Times obituary, looking back to the '30s, had him as 'certainly the purest produced in England at that time.'

Endnotes

1   Herbert Read, 'A Nest of Gentle Artists', *Apollo*, September 1962.

2   'Mondrian in London', *Studio International*, December 1962.

3   Geoffrey Grigson, 'Painting and Sculpture', in Geoffrey Grigson (ed.), *The Arts Today*, London, p.75, 1935.

4   John Constable, letter to John Fisher, 26 August 1827.

5   John Keats, letter to his brother George, 11 April 1819.

6   Quoted by Andrew Saint in *Belsize 2000: A Living Suburb*, Belsize Conservation Area Advisory Committee.

7   *Letters of Roger Fry*, edited by Denys Sutton, Chatto & Windus, 1972, letters to Helen Anrep, Paris, 1 May 1925, and G.L. Dickinson, Vichy, 16 September 1927.

8   'The Future of Painting', *The Listener*, 2 October 1935.

9   *Letters of Roger Fry*, edited by Denys Sutton, Chatto & Windus, 1972, letter, 3 November 1928.

10   *op cit*, Letter to Vanessa Bell, 14 December 1921.

11   R.H. Wilenski, *The Modern Movement in Art*, Faber & Gwyer, 1927.

12   Herbert Read, 'A Nest of Gentle Artists', *Apollo*, September 1962.

13   'Moving into the Mall Studios: Lady Read talks to Leonie Cohn', *Belsize 2000: a living suburb*, Belsize Conservation Area Advisory Committee.

14   Wednesday, 20 February 1935, *The Diary of Virginia Woolf, Volume IV, 1931-35*, edited by Anne Olivier Bell, The Hogarth Press, 1982.

15   *Letters of Roger Fry*, edited by Denys Sutton, Chatto & Windus, 1972, letter to Lady Read.

16   Herbert Read, *The Meaning of Art*, Faber & Faber, 1931.

17   Quoted without reference in George Woodcock, *Herbert Read: The Stream and the Source*, 1972.

18   Herbert Read, *A Concise History of Modern Painting*, Thames & Hudson, 1959.

19   Herbert Read, *The Meaning of Art*, Faber & Faber, 1931.

20   *Letters of Roger Fry*, edited by Denys Sutton, Chatto & Windus, 1972, letter to Helen Anrep, c.1928.

21   *op cit*, letter to Kenneth Clark, 4 August 1933.

22   *Listener*, 24 September 1932.

23   *Spectator*, 2 August 1940.

24   Margaret Gardiner, *A Scatter of Memories*, Free Association Books, London, 1988. (Margaret saw to it that the birth of triplets to Barbara Hepworth in 1934 did not prevent her from continuing to make sculpture.)

25   Geoffrey Grigson, *Recollections: Mainly of Writers and Artists*, Chatto and Windus, London, 1984.

26   Naum Gabo talking to Maurice de Sausmarez in 'Ben Nicholson', special edition of *Studio International*, 1969.

27   Margaret Gardiner, *A Scatter of Memories*, Free Association Books, London, 1988.

28   *op cit*.

29   Herbert Read, 'A Nest of Gentle Artists', *Apollo*, 1962.

30   Herbert Read, 'The Faculty of Abstraction', *Circle: international survey of constructive art*, edited by J.L. Martin, Ben Nicholson, N. Gabo, Faber and Faber, 1937.

31   Adrian Stokes, *Colour and Form*, Faber and Faber, 1937.

32   Roger Fry, 'The Artist and Psycho-Analysis', Hogarth Press, 1924, originally a paper read to the British Psychological Society. Published in *Roger Fry, Art and Market: Roger Fry on Commerce in Art*, edited by Craufurd D. Goodwin, foreword by Asa Briggs, The University of Michigan Press, 1999.

33   33   J.M. Richards, 'The Condition of Architecture and the Principle of Anonymity', *Circle: international survey of constructive art*, edited by J.L. Martin, Ben Nicholson, N. Gabo, Faber and Faber, 1937.

34   *op cit*, Editorial, pV.

35   Eric Gill, essays.

36   Barbara Hepworth, 'Sculpture', *Circle: international survey of constructive art*, edited by J.L. Martin, Ben Nicholson, N. Gabo, Faber and Faber, 1937.

37   Naum Gabo in *Studio International*, December 1966.

38   Letter to Ben Nicholson, September 1934.

39   *Listener*, 2 and 23 October 1935.

40   Kenneth Clark, *Another Part of the Wood: A Self-Portrait*, John Murray, 1970.

41   'Living Art in England', London Gallery, January 1939, included work by Gabo, Mondrian, Hepworth, Nicholson, Stephenson, Piper and others. Moore exhibited as a 'surrealist'. They also exhibited under such labels at Bernheim Jeune in May in 'Abstract and Concrete Art', a show which included Calder, Van Doesburg, Kandinsky, Arp, Taeuber-Arp, Vantongerloo and others.

42   Letter 27 November 1937.

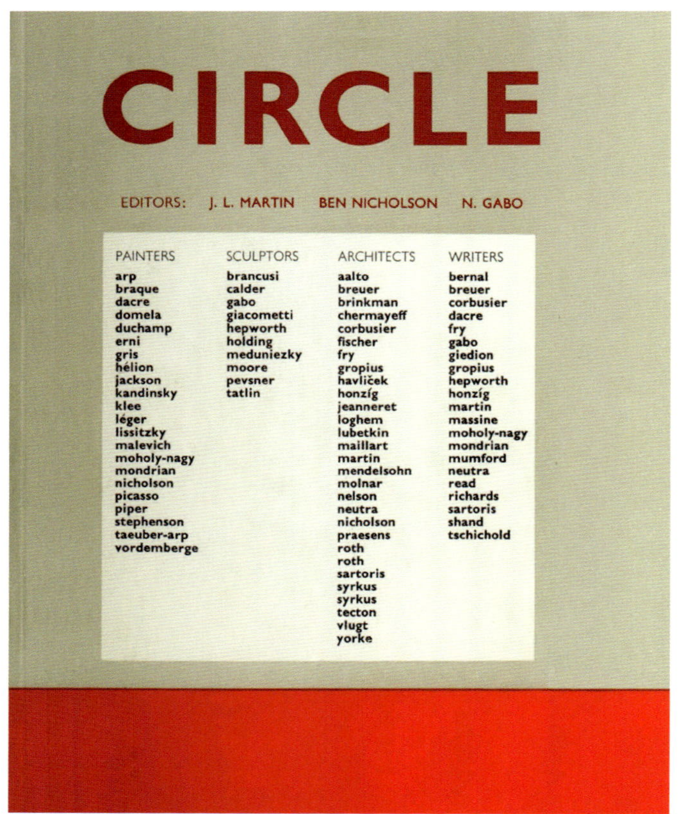

Fig. 21 – Cover of paperback version (1971) of *Circle: International Survey of Constructivist Art*. Published by Faber & Faber in 1937, it was edited by the artists Ben Nicholson and Naum Gabo and the architect Leslie Martin with the layout being designed by Barbara Hepworth. *Circle* was intended to be a series of publications so is sometimes referred to as a journal or magazine, although only one issue was actually produced due to the outbreak of World War II.

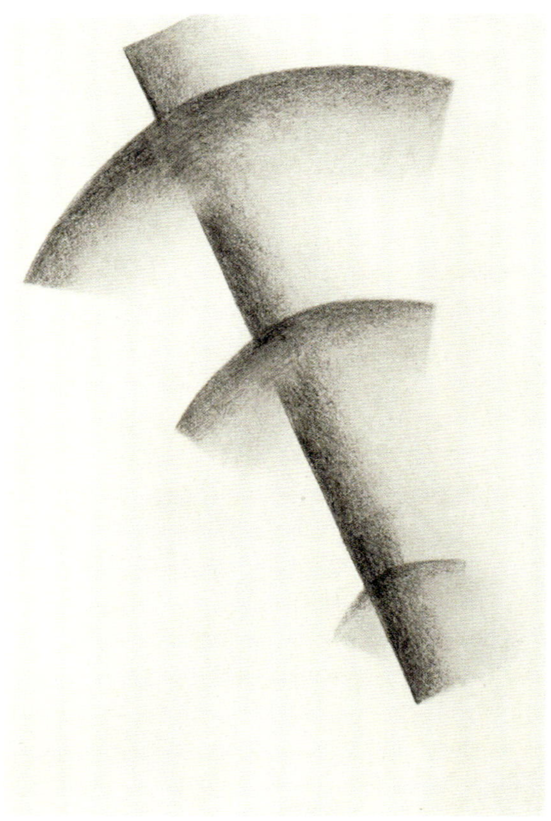

Fig. 22 – Kazimir Malevich (1879-1935)
Suprematistic composition – White in white.
(Feeling of fading away), 1916,
This work opened the painting section of *Circle*.

John Cecil Stephenson (1889-1965)
Pioneer of Abstraction

Peyton Skipwith

*'Execution and technique play an important part in the aim of establishing
a more or less objective vision which the essence of the non-figurative work demands.'*

Mondrian in his essay 'Plastic Art and Pure Plastic Art (Figurative Art and Non-Figurative Art)" in *Circle,*
the Manifesto publishedto coincide with the exhibition of Constructive Art at the London Gallery in July 1937.

Cecil Stephenson was one of the pioneers of abstract art in England, along with Ben Nicholson, Barbara Hepworth, Henry Moore, John Piper, Edward Wadsworth and half-a-dozen others. This move towards abstraction had two principal strands, one leaning towards surrealism and the other to geometric abstraction, or Constructivism as it came to be known.[1] Stephenson and his friends were mostly in the latter camp, and the London Gallery's exhibition drew them together along with a distinguished group of foreign exhibitors including Moholy-Nagy, Calder, Giacometti, Hélion and Naum Gabo.

Circle (**Fig. 21**), edited by Leslie Martin, Ben Nicholson and Naum Gabo is more than a manifesto, it is a book nearly three hundred pages long, divided into sections on 'Painting', 'Sculpture', 'Architecture' and 'Art and Life', with essays by Le Corbusier, Herbert Read, Naum Gabo and Marcel Breuer among others. The sequence of reproductions in the 'Painting' section opens with a 1916 work by Malevitch (**Fig. 22**): it is, of course, essentially non-figurative, but consists of a central rod with three arcs in descending sizes, giving the impression that it is part of some vital – in every sense of the word – piece of machinery. Apart from an early Cubist work by Picasso and a 1918 Leger, it is the nearest that any of the illustrated works gets to being an interpretation of a tangible object.

Just as Mondrian began his journey towards non-figuration through the modification and simplification of forms, natural and man-made – branches of trees and elements of church architecture – so Stephenson began his through isolating and refining industrial elements – cogs, axles, wheels, pistons, etc – derived from the multiple pieces of machinery he managed to house within his Hampstead studio. J.D. Bernal, another contributor to *Circle*, in his essay 'Art and the Scientist', analysing the problem faced by Constructivists in the formalisation of content in painting, drew attention to the possible use of forms 'such as occur in modern engineering practice, but with a strong tendency to geometricization and abstraction.'[2] He could have been writing directly about Stephenson's early 'thirties paintings; however, the painting chosen by the editors of *Circle* to illustrate his work, *Six Elements*, (1937), had moved as far aesthetically from such works as *The Pump* (1932), *The Lathe* (1933) and *Mechanism* (**Cat. 6**) of 1934 as *Mechanism* had from the 1919 naturalistic portrait of Ethel Brown. In the eighteen years that separate this directly observed and sympathetic portrait of his friend Gregory Brown's young daughter from *Six Elements*, Stephenson had travelled from naturalism through abstraction to geometric non-figuration. A logical and satisfying journey, but it wasn't to end there. The War years brought him back again to more direct raportage with scenes of the blitz, including *The End of a Doodlebug* (**CAT. 19**), which he exhibited at the Royal Academy in 1944, then, post-war, under the influence of Abstract Expressionism and Tachism, he was to immerse himself once again in total non-figuration. (**Fig. 23**) This time, though, texture rather than geometry was to become the overriding feature, and, during a final burst of creative activity in the late 'fifties, he produced a startling series of brightly coloured and aggressively impastoed canvases, before a near-fatal stroke brought to an end his painting career.

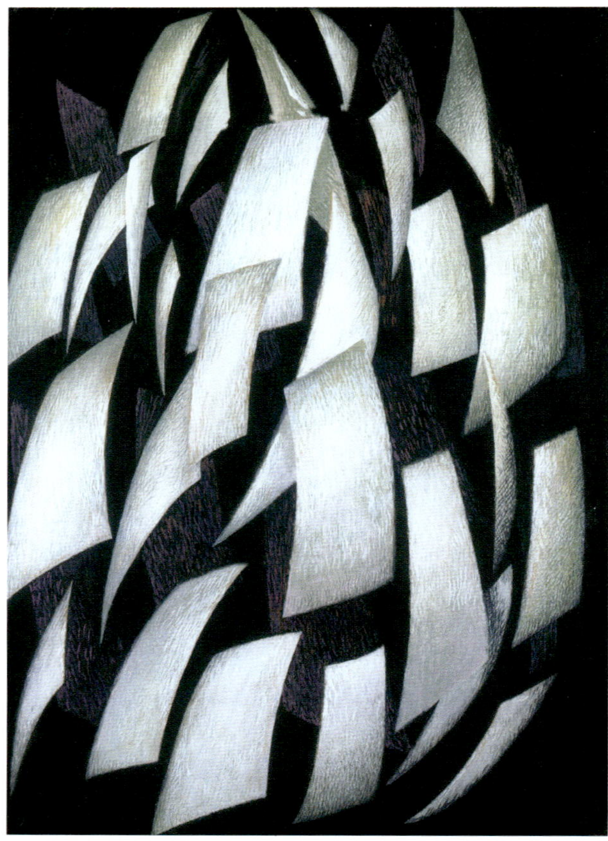

Fig. 23 – *Rondo (A Nous la Liberté)*, 1953, signed verso. tempera on board, 32 × 24 in. (81.5 × 61 cm).

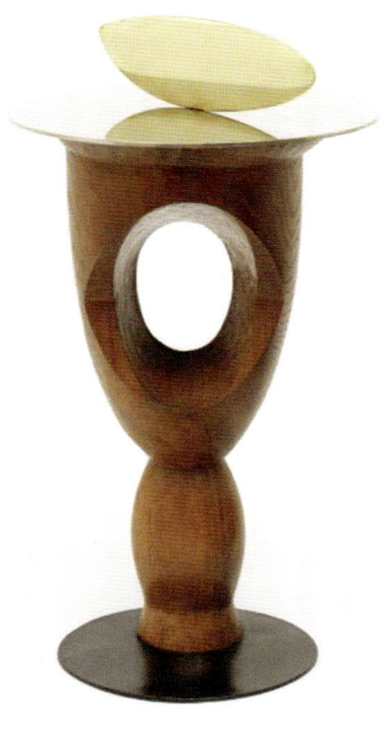

If Stephenson had been born fifteen or twenty years earlier he would have been an ideal recruit to that band of artists who clustered around the Arts and Crafts Movement. His lifelong fascination with making and repairing things, coupled with his obliviousness to time and the cost of materials, is akin to those same qualities manifested by W.A.S. Benson and that gentle dreamer Edward Johnston.[3] Johnston always had pockets full of string and sealing wax, tools and sandpaper, ready to immerse himself in any diverting task, oblivious of the main job in hand. Stephenson, only seventeen years his junior, turned, with equal enthusiasm and wholehearted concentration, to making and repairing, but utilising machine tools rather than handcraft. The large-scale model engine, the 'Aberdonian', which he built, was strong enough to take the weight of two grown men, whilst Jim Ede entrusted him with repairing a sculpture, *Fish* (**Fig. 24**), which Guthrie[4] ascribes to Brancusi, but was more likely Gaudier-Brzeska's *Bird Swallowing a Fish*, one of the few works to have been cast in Gaudier's lifetime. Like Johnston, Stephenson would have subscribed to Lethaby's dictum that 'A work of art is a well-made thing, that is all. It may be a well-made statue or a well-made chair, or a well-made book. Art is not a special sauce applied to ordinary cooking; it is the cooking itself if it is good. Most simply and generally art may be thought of as the well-doing of what needs doing.'[5]

What were the driving impulses behind his aesthetic development? And what is his place in history? To answer these questions it is necessary to look back at his early life and training, as well as those accidental circumstances arising from his service in the munitions industry during the Great War, and later serendipitous meetings with Hampstead neighbours.

John Cecil Stephenson, known to his family as Cecil, and to other friends such as Ben Nicholson as Stevo or Stevoe, was born in Bishop Auckland, County Durham in 1889; his father was an ostler and, later, inn-keeper's assistant, who, by dint of hard work saved enough money to enable him to open a small grocery shop shortly before the outbreak of the Great War. The typical reaction of a working class family at that period to the thought of a son of theirs going to art school would have been 'that's not for the likes of us lad.' When Charles Sargeant Jagger, a near contemporary, was seen by his father carving a piece of stone, he was sent into the garden to cut the hedge, with the comment 'that will teach you to make things into shape.'[6] Jagger never dared tell his father, until after the event, that he had applied for a scholarship to the Royal College of Art. However, Robert Stephenson and his wife, Elizabeth, were clearly more broadminded than Enoch Jagger and were pleased, within their limited financial means, to foster their son's ambitions. Their eldest son, Alfred, had settled in France and worked for a large export company, so they were able to concentrate on Cecil, who was both musical and artistic.[7] From the local primary school he went to the Art School at Darlington Technical College, before winning a scholarship to Leeds College of Art, remaining there until 1914 when a second scholarship enabled him to go, like Jagger, to the Royal College of Art in London. He was not entirely happy at the College, but a further scholarship the following year allowed him to transfer to the Slade. A remarkable progression.

With the prolongation of the War his period at the Slade was curtailed, and he moved back to Bishop Auckland, working first of all at Tilney's Engineering Works and then at The Old Forge on the production of munitions. After eight years as an art student the contrast of heavy manufacturing industry was largely beneficial. As Simon Guthrie says, 'the munitions work provided Stephenson with an insight into structures and construction, which in the long term affected his view of Art in a positive manner. The uncanny speed and precision with which a billet of metal could be transformed into an object of utility fascinated him. He also found that he was very good at doing this. Looking round he could see that the shapes of lathes, milling machines and routers, had a purposive beauty which depended on a strict relationship between their constituent parts, dictated solely by function.'[8]

Cecil had begun to sell works whilst still a student and had also built up a local Bishop Auckland clientele for portrait commissions (**Cat. 3**); these works were strictly traditional in terms of execution, as can be judged from the slightly later portrait of Ethel Brown, but he would also have been aware of more modern trends. Frank Rutter, a champion of Post-Impressionism, had been appointed Director of Leeds City Art Gallery during Cecil's time at the College, whilst Michael Sadler, the first Principal of Leeds University was a collector of works by members of the New English Art Club and, along with his son, an early advocate of Kandinsky's work, which he had first seen at Rutter's Allied Artists Association exhibition at the Albert Hall in 1911.[9]

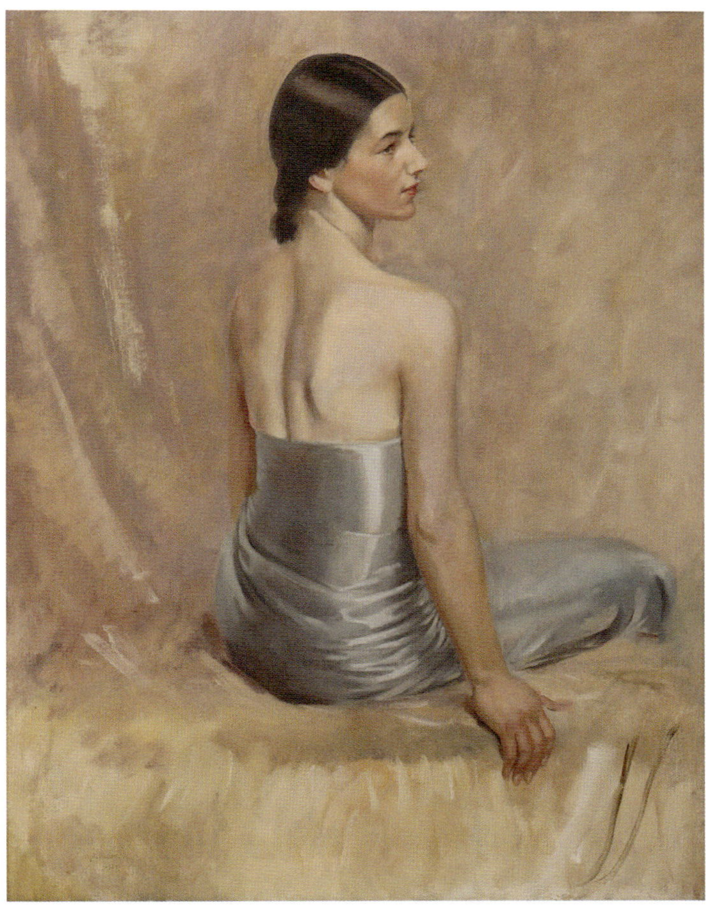

Moving back to London after the War Stephenson made contact with friends from the Royal College and the Slade, and was also introduced to Sickert, who, he reported to his family, 'liked my drawings very much indeed,' and encouraged him to get a studio. This he did, installing himself at the end of March 1919 in No.6, The Mall, Parkhill Road, Hampstead, which was to remain his home for the rest of his life. Although during his early years in the Mall Studios his finances were dire and he was often lonely and despondent, as time went by it was to prove a particularly fortuitous choice; in 1927, Barbara Hepworth and her then husband, John Skeaping, moved into No.7 and the following year Herbert Read joined them at No.3. Henry Moore and Ben Nicholson were also living nearby in Parkhill Road, and during the following decade this 'gentle nest of artists' as Read described it was joined by Naum Gabo, Mondrian, Hans Erni and Hélion. Also, by 1933 Nicholson had replaced Skeaping as Hepworth's partner and was ensconced immediately next door at No.7. Stephenson's finances had also improved slightly due to his appointment as Head of the Art Department in the School of Surveying and Building at the Northern Polytechnic in Holloway Road in 1922.

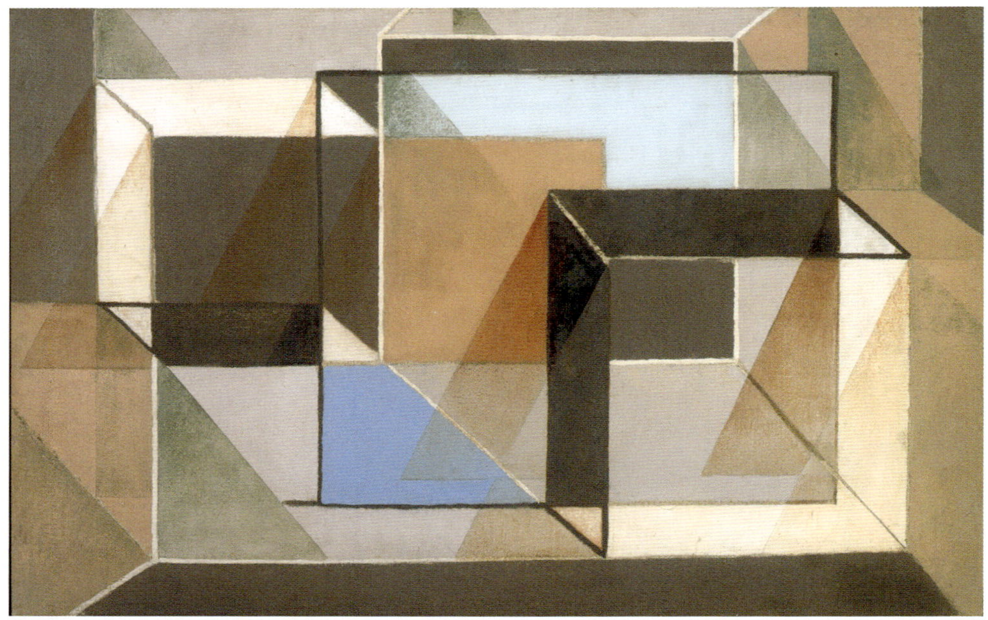

Fig. 25 – *Interpenetration I*, 1934, signed and dated verso,
oil on canvas, 36 × 23 in. (91.5 × 58.5 cm).
Literature: Simon Gutherie, *John Cecil Stephenson*, 1997; The Fine Art Society, *John Cecil Stephenson*, 2007.

By 1933 Stephenson had already turned his back on the straightforward landscapes and portraits, which had attracted his early patrons from County Durham, and embarked on the series of simplified and stylised machine paintings, of which *Mechanism* (**Cat. 6**) is a fine example. The hard, mechanical forms in these paintings are refined and pared away to their constituent parts.[10] The arrival of Ben Nicholson in the adjacent studio at this time was particularly fortuitous; they had each separately started blurring the boundary between figuration and abstraction, and were now engaged on exploring the potential of pure form free of reference to the tangible world. In Stephenson's small panel, *Abstraction* painted that same year, 1933, it is tempting to see the first evidence of a neighbourly exchange of views and cross-fertilisation of ideas. The shapes are no longer either referential or structural but float freely in space; the powder blues, whites, charcoal and chewing-gum browns of *Mechanism* have been joined by ochre and crimson, which, along with sage green, was to remain his basic palette throughout the decade, though the intensity of colour varied. Stephenson's regular contact with architects at the Polytechnic helped stimulate his interest in space and spacial relationships, adding an extra optical dimension to his work at this time; not only do shapes float in space they interweave one with another creating an extraordinary sense of progression and recession. This is particularly apparent in both *Interpenetration I* of 1934 (**Fig. 25**) and *Nine Uprights* painted three years later. In *Interpenetration I* Stephenson plays with perspective through the overlayering of cubes, part opaque, part transparent, thus manipulating the sense of space: in this he anticipates Gabo who, in his article 'Construction in Space', writes about the 'space in which the mass exists made visible.'[11] Gabo was, naturally, thinking three-dimensionally rather than illusionistically, but the effect is the same, and to illustrate his article he chose two contrasting plywood cubes.; one solid and box-like, the other open, consisting of an X frame with a top and base, thus revealing the space within.[12]

The Nazi terror may have, briefly, enriched the community around Mall Studios with the arrival of Gabo, Mondrian (**Fig. 26**), Erni and Hélion, but this was only temporary; the refugees duly departed in search of more permanent homes, Read had already moved to Buckinghamshire and, with the outbreak of war, Ben and Barbara and their children left for St Ives. Only Stephenson remained. Whilst the Nicholsons retained No. 3, Henry Moore later took over the lease of No. 7, which he retained until his death; Bernard Meadows used it intermittently but, during the war years at least, Moore and his family were based at Much Hadham. Despite air raids and bombing, which did considerable collateral damage to the Studios, Stephenson was able to go on living there, spending many nights fire-watching from the roof of the Polytechnic, where he was still teaching. Ben and Barbara wrote frequently from Cornwall, often their letters were concerned entirely with domestic affairs concerning the safety of the studio, or with the fate of mutual friends – Mondrian, Hélion and Gabo particularly – but in January 1941 Ben wrote exhorting him that 'We must affirm that abstract painting is a new dimension of plastic creativity: an invention that affects the kind & not merely the quality of painting. Again it is still a tentative & experimental art which has an immense capacity for growth & achievement. It, too, is an art of the future – if there is to be a future.'[13] Despite this pessimistic ending, Nicholson was still able to do some work and, later, would consult Stephenson with regard to materials, glues, etc., to assist in the making of his constructions.

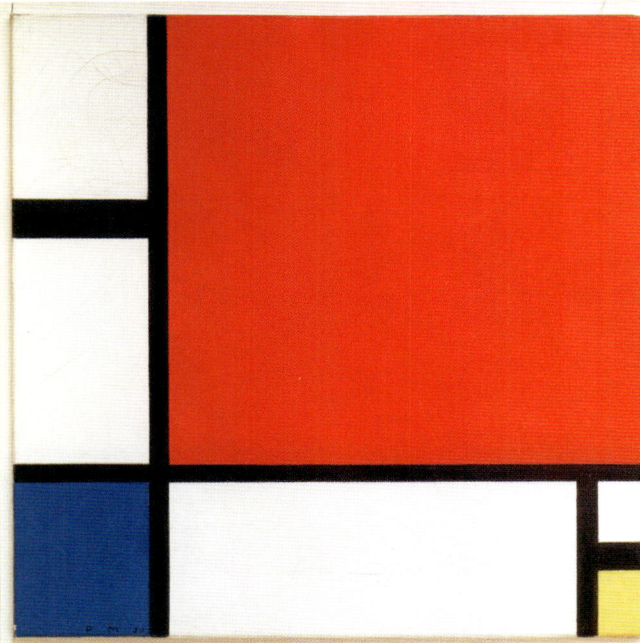

Fig. 26 – Piet Mondrian (1872-1944), *Composition with Red, Blue, and Yellow,* 1930, oil on canvas, 18 × 18 in. (46 × 46 cm). Collection: Kunsthaus Zürich.

Post-war recovery was slow, but Stephenson was lucky to still have his job at the Polytechnic, to which he had remained loyal despite approaches from other more prestigious institutions, then, in 1950 he received the commission to produce a ceiling painting for a corridor within the Industry Building for the Festival of Britain. Although the commission was welcome the location and elevated position of the work was not ideal. For this work, to be executed in luminous paints, he reverted to pre-war geometric ideas, though the patterning became consciously two- rather than three-dimensional; the last thing visitors wished to be conscious of whilst passing along the corridor was a vision of concrete forms bearing down on their heads. A few years later, in 1955, he was approached by a young architect on the staff of the Northern Polytechnic, Bill Curtis, with a proposal to provide a mural, iron staircase and central fire-grate for a house he was building at Rickmansworth in Hertfordshire. Solar House, as it was called, was of a revolutionary design and received considerable coverage in the architectural press. The mural, now removed, like that for the Festival of Britain, is of a geometrical design, but the forms have become rounder, fatter and generally more substantial, filling the entire surface. A development anticipated in such works as *Chromatic* of the previous year, picking up on some of the visual ideas Hélion had been experimenting with in the 1930s in his attempt to define 'shallow space'. As a result of this, the kinetic quality of his earlier work was replaced by a new solidity.

The 1950s was a decade of fresh opportunities and experimentation: although due to the general economic situation individual collectors were few and far between, there was the promise of public patronage both from the state and private sectors, and a new awareness of the demand for art for public spaces.

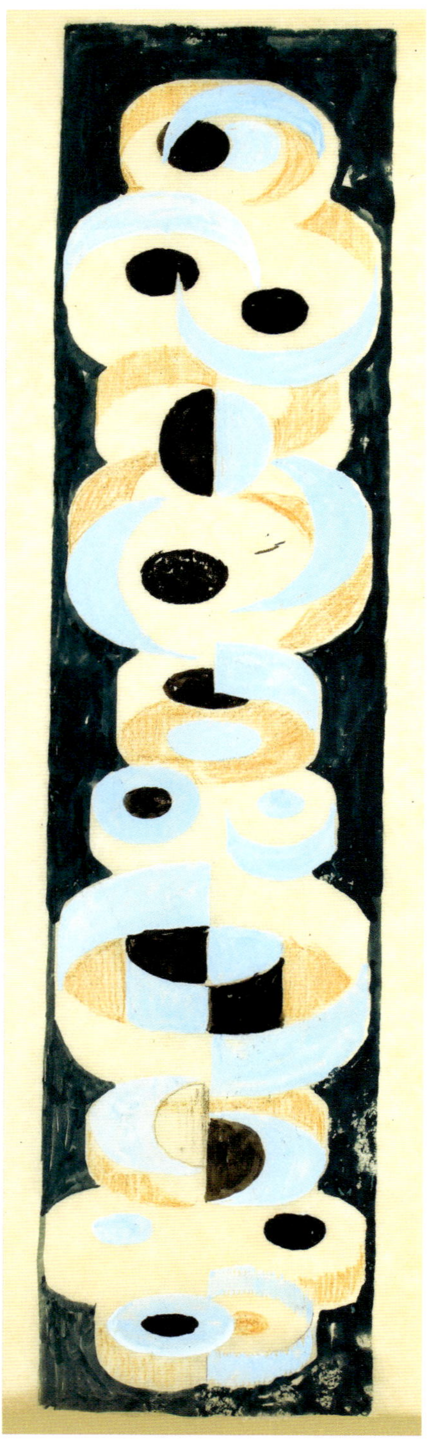

CAT. 4 – Preliminary study for plyglass mural, Queen Mary's College, signed, inscribed with title and dated in pen & ink, gouache, crayon and pencil, on tracing paper; 21 ¼ × 5 ½ in. (54 × 14 cm). Provenance: Marjorie Guthrie.

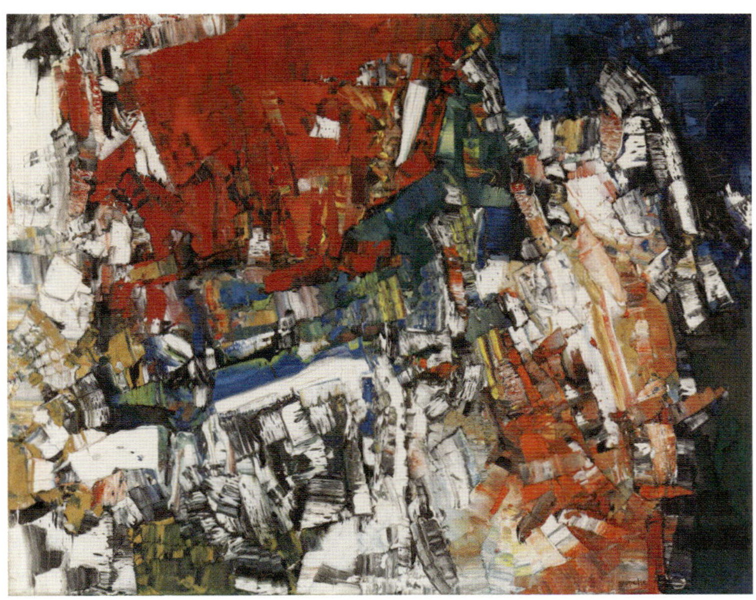

Fig. 27 – Jean-Paul Riopelle (1923-2002), *Perspectives,* 1956,
oil on canvas, 31 ¾ × 39 ½ in. (80.6 × 100 cm). Collection: Tate.

Stephenson responded to the challenge. In addition to the Festival of Britain and Curtis's Solar House, he received a commission from one of the many new start-up companies, Plyglass Ltd., manufacturers of laminated glass, asking him to produce a series of designs for panels to show off their new material. In all he produced about a score of designs ranging from *Sketch for Ply Glass,* 1957, with its sensation of black leading and a diapering of brightly coloured lozenges, reminiscent of sheets hanging out to dry on the balconies of some Mediterranean tenement block, to the decorative panels for the new Engineering Block at Queen Mary College, University of London (**CAT. 4, 27**) and the 170 foot long geometrical facia panel for the British Industrial Pavilion at the 1958 Brussels Exposition (**Fig. 20**). Perhaps inspired by the wider possibilities of laminated glass, he produced alongside these more tightly controlled designs, his final series of Tachist-inspired paintings including *Dorian.* Whilst his non-figurative geometric works of the 1930s have the restraint of classic English good taste, these late paintings bear the hallmarks of Abstract Expressionism and are unashamedly and exuberantly executed in the International style of the 1950s (**Fig. 27**). They are redolent of that decade which witnessed a new, young generation of European painters emerge from the ravages of war, starvation and post-war rationing, with an ineluctable lust for life, and a perception of New York rather than Paris as the fountainhead of vital contemporary art.

What Stephenson had achieved in his 1930s paintings such as *Interpenetration 1, Nine Uprights* and *Six Elements 1,* illustrated in *Circle,* was not only a sense of depth and three-dimensionality, but also a sense of movement, an illusion that anticipated Op Art by some thirty years. He further exploited this illusory sense of motion during the remainder of the decade, gradually

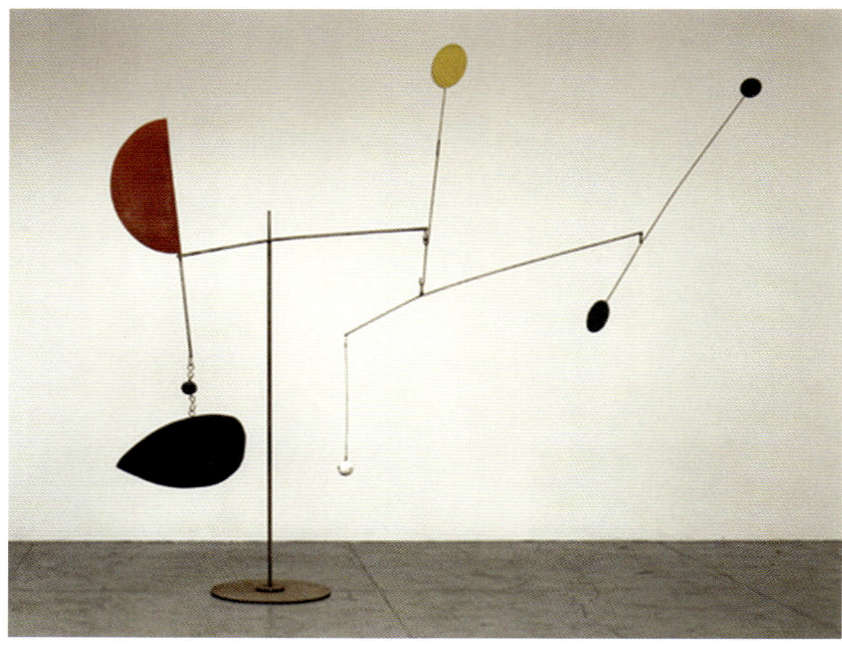

Fig. 28 – Alexander Calder (1898-1978), *Steel Fish*,1934,
sheet metal, 115 × 137 × 120 in. (292 × 348 × 304.8 cm). Calder Foundation, New York.

moving on from rigidly geometric forms to embrace both curves and irregular shapes. The sketch for *Six Curved Forms* of 1938 and *Vortex* of the following year, explore two-dimensionally the same optical material that Alexander Calder was treating in his mobiles (**Fig. 28**). It cannot be coincidental that one of the two Calder mobiles illustrate in *Circle*, dating from 1935 and 1936, belonged to Ben Nicholson, and was thus in the neighbouring studio.[14] There is absolutely no doubt that during the 1930s Stephenson was both geographically and aesthetically at the very heart of British Modernism. Ideas flowed backwards and forwards, not just between the studios but across national boundaries. Postwar, although perhaps no longer in the avant-garde, he still remained within the mainstream producing work of an international dimension.

Geometric non-figuration was at its zenith in the mid-1930s and Stephenson was at the forefront of the movement. If some individuals are better known than others, it has as much – if not more – to do with personalities as achievements.[15] Stephenson, conscious of his Northern working-class roots, had always retained a certain detachment from cosmopolitan artistic circles. By temperament, if not necessarily by choice, he remained something of an outsider. The fact that this restraint in no way detracted from his achievements is clearly borne out by Read's recognition that he was 'one of the earliest artists in this country to develop a completely abstract style'.[16] His 1937 egg tempera *Painting* more than holds its own alongside works by his international peers from the Circle group – Moholy-Nagy, Gabo, Hélion and Calder, as well as with those by Ben and Winifred Nicholson, Piper, Moore and Hepworth.

Endnotes

1   'In the late thirties, as it became increasingly clear that there were forms of abstract art which were incompatible with the kind of work published in *Circle,* 'Constructive' came to replace 'abstract' as a means of self-identification for those opposed to Surrealist influence.' Charles Harrison, *English Art and Modernism 1900-1939,* Allen Lane / Indiana University Press, 1981, p.287.

2   *Circle,* Faber & Faber, 1937, p.122.

3   Edward Johnston, 1872–1944, almost single-handedly revived the art of calligraphy. He designed and made a water-clock to open his chicken-house in the mornings as well as a pump to irrigate his Thames-side garden, whilst the toys he devised for his children were works of pure genius.

4   Simon Guthrie, *John Cecil Stephenson*, Cartmel Press,1997, p.68.

5   *Imprint,* July 1913. For extra emphasis Lethaby printed the last six words of this quote in large capitals.

6   Ann Compton, *Charles Sargeant Jagger,* The Henry Moore Foundation in association with Lund Humphries, 2004, p.12.

7   Jasia Reichardt, in her introductory essay *Musical Abstractions* to the catalogue of Fischer Fine Art's 1976 Stephenson exhibition wrote: 'Stephenson occupies a special place in the avant-garde movement of the 1930s. There is one very specific reason for this. He drew inspiration from music and architecture and these are the essential and inevitable qualities which his work conveys.'

8   Guthrie, op. cit., p.22.

9   See Tom Steele, *Alfred Orage and The Leeds Art Club 1893-1923*, Scolar Press, 1990, p179–80.

10   This concentration during the early 'thirties on isolating mechanical parts may have been stimulated, at least in part, by Paul Strand's photographs such as *Motion Picture Camera.* Harold Clurman describes the machine in Strand's photographs as having in some mysterious way 'become conscious of its own admirable and independent life, its own elegance of line, suave hardness and density of substance.' *The Studio,* Vol. 98, 1929, pp.735–8.

11   *Circle,* op.cit., p.106.

12   Gabo presented these cubes to the Tate Gallery and they are currently on display at Tate Britain in Gallery 22, along with other Constructivist works relating to *Circle.*

13   Letter 7, 12 January 1941, Tate Archive.

14   Calder produced a number of such mobiles at this time, and Marjorie Guthrie recalls one hanging in 6 Mall Studios, which is not surprising, considering that the second London performance of Calder's 'Circus' was performed there to an admiring audience of Nicholsons, Gabo, et al. See Simon Guthrie, *John Cecil Stephenson* and Sarah Jane Checkland, *Ben Nicholson: The Vicious Circles of his Life and Art.*

15   Herbert Read wrote in his Introduction to the catalogue of Stephenson's 1960 Drian Gallery exhibition: 'The vicissitudes of the art world are such that it is possible for an artist of great talent to work for a lifetime in obscurity, and only towards the end of his career find the recognition that is due to him.' Extraordinarily, despite the fact that he had been working for over forty years, this was Stephenson's first one-man exhibition.

16   Ibid.

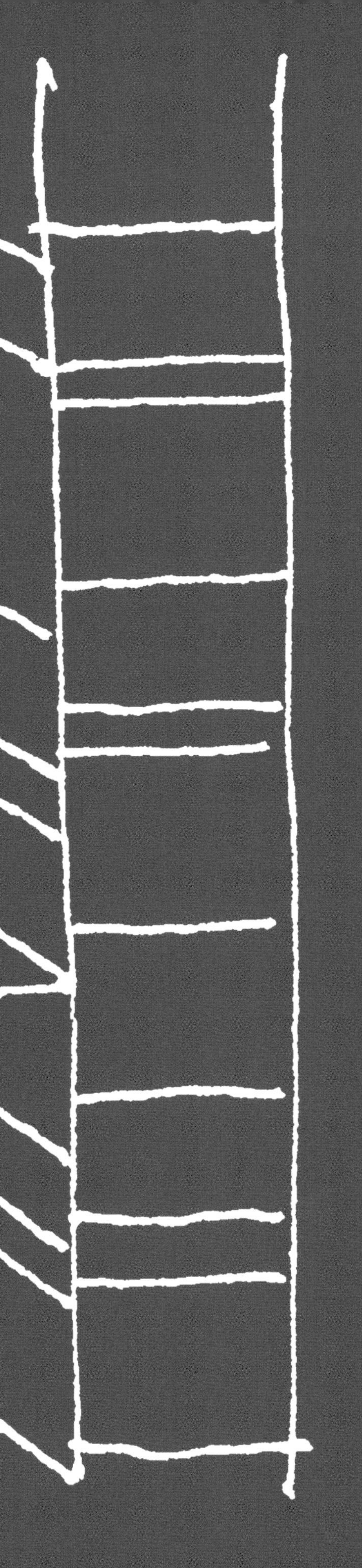

CATALOGUE

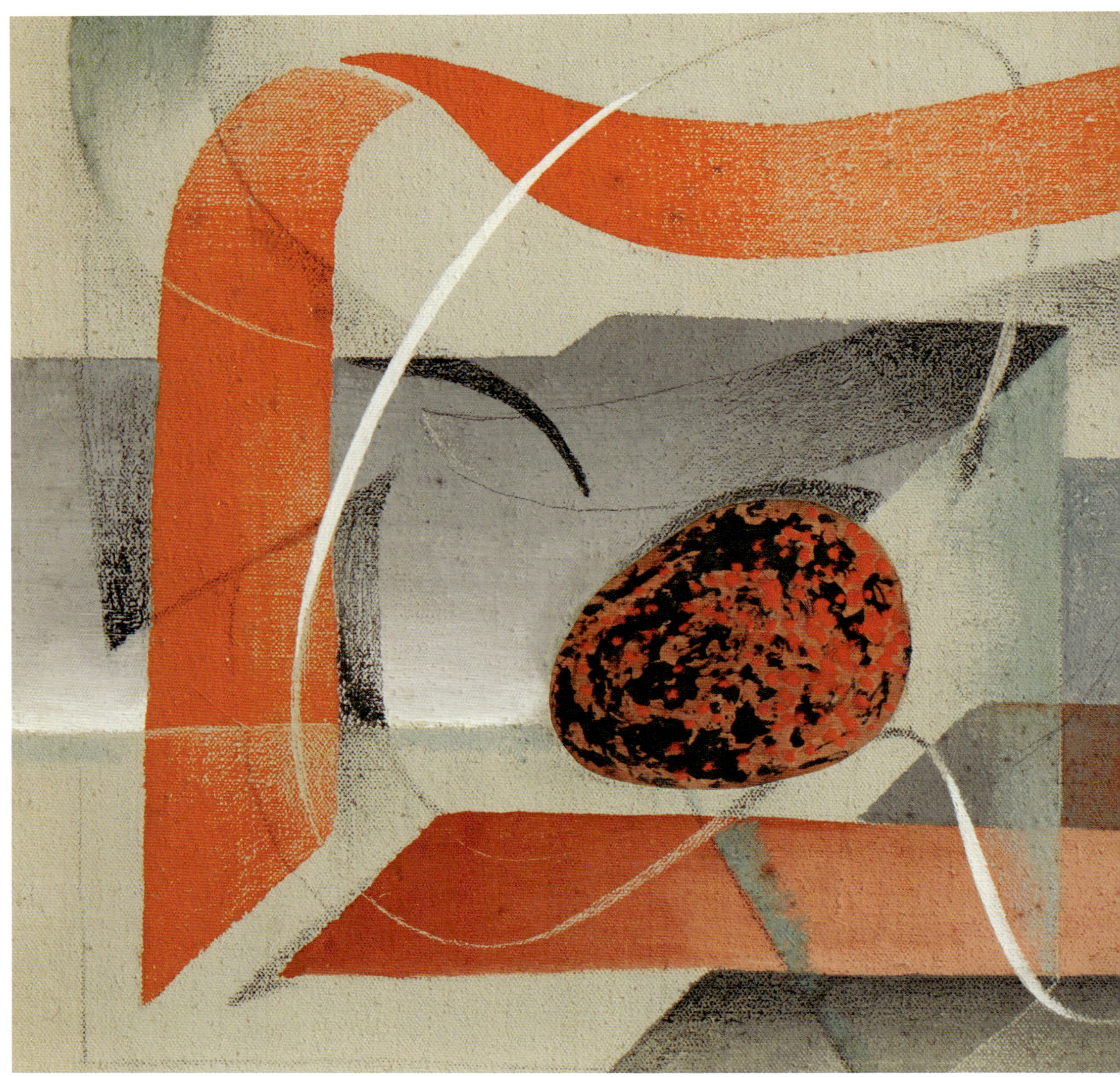

CAT. 5 – *Abstraction*, 1934,
signed twice and inscribed and dated 'JC STEPHENSON/1934/CECIL STEPHENSON/6 MALL STUDIOS/HAMPSTEAD NW3' (on the reverse).
oil, gouache, pencil and collage on canvas over panel, 9 × 18 ¼ in. (23 × 46 cm).
Provenance: John Bruckland. His sale; Christie's, London, 26 March 1993, lot 1, where purchased by Dr Jeffrey Sherwin.

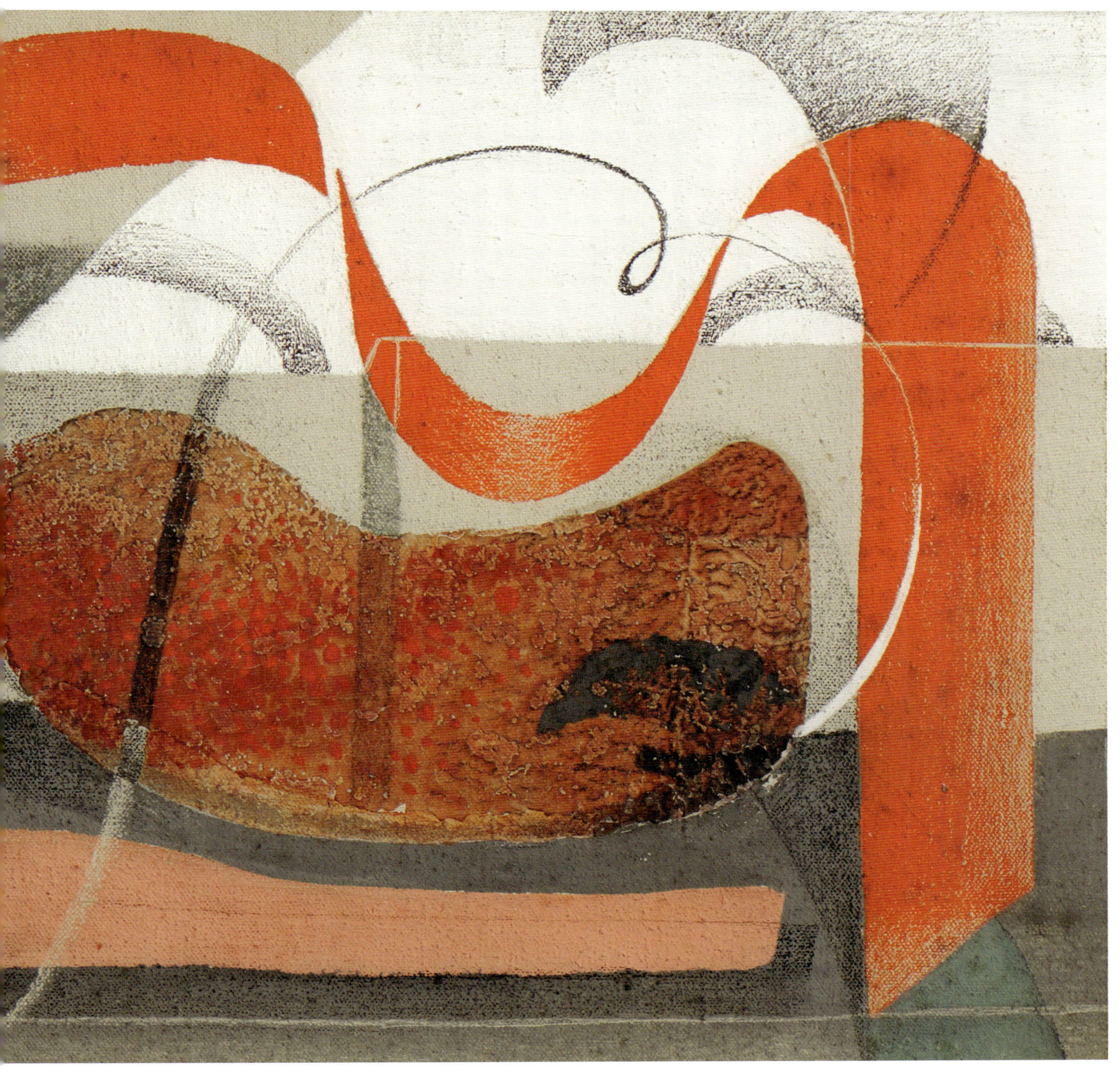

Exhibition: London, Fischer Fine Art, *Cecil Stephenson 1889-1965*, October - November 1976, no. 16, as 'Painting'. London, Fine Art Society, *John Cecil Stephenson*, October - November 2007, no. 14.
Literature: *John Cecil Stephenson*, Simon Guthrie, 1997; *John Cecil Stephenson*, The Fine Art Society in association with Paul Liss, catalogue number 14; *John Cecil Stephenson – Pioneer of Modernism*, Conor Mullan, DLI Museum and Art Gallery, 2012.

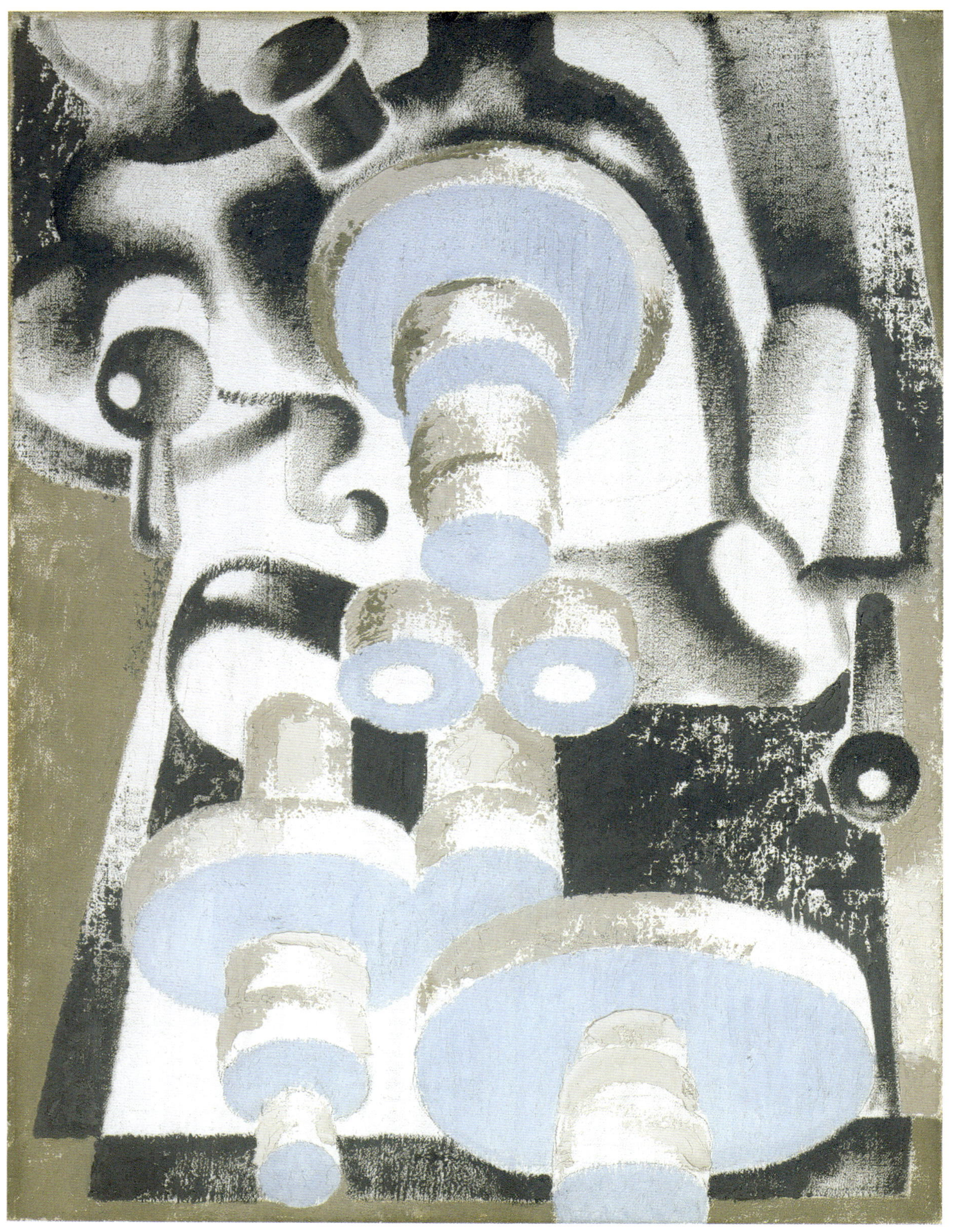

CAT. 6 — *The Mechanism*, 1933,
oil on canvas on board, 18 × 14 inches (45.7 × 35.5 cm).
Exhibited: The Fine Art Society, 2007.
Literature: Simon Guthrie, *John Cecil Stephenson*, 1997, (28) illustrated page 146.

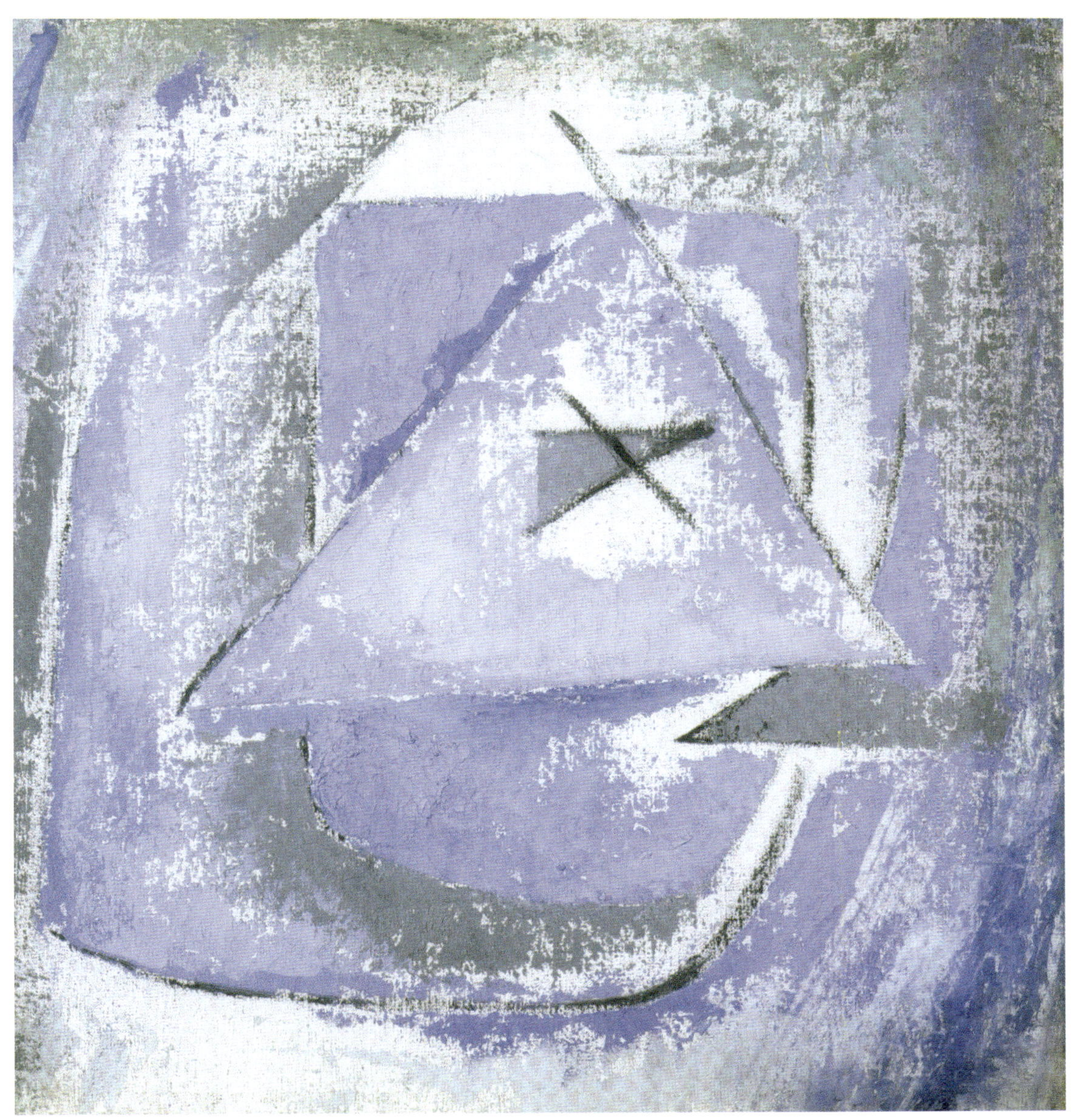

CAT. 7 – *Mask,* 1934, signed and dated verso,
oil on canvas on board, 13 × 13 inches (33 × 33 cm).
Exhibited: London Leicester Galleries, 7 & 5 Sciety, 1934; Camden Arts Centre, 1975; The Fine Art Society, 2007, n° 4.
Literature: Simon Guthrie, *John Cecil Stephenson*, 1997, (29) illustrated page 146.

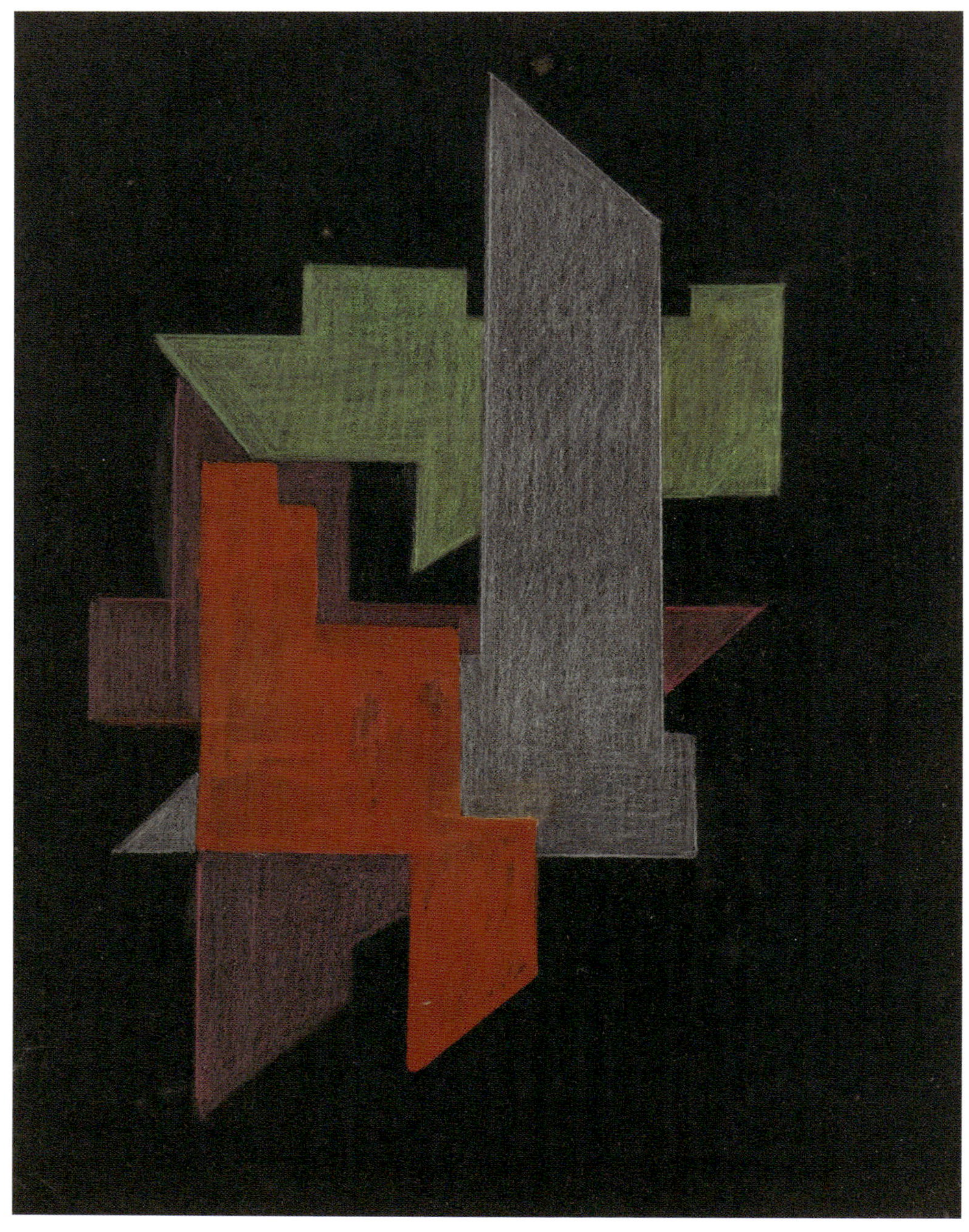

CAT. 8 – *Uprights, 1936/37, signed, dated and titled to label on reverse, gouache and crayon on paper, 9 ½ x 7 ¾ in. (24 x 19.5 cm). Provenance: The Artists Family.*

CAT. 9 – *Concrete Composition, gouache and collage on tracing paper over ink on paper, 12 x 7 ¼ in. (30 x 18.5 cm).*

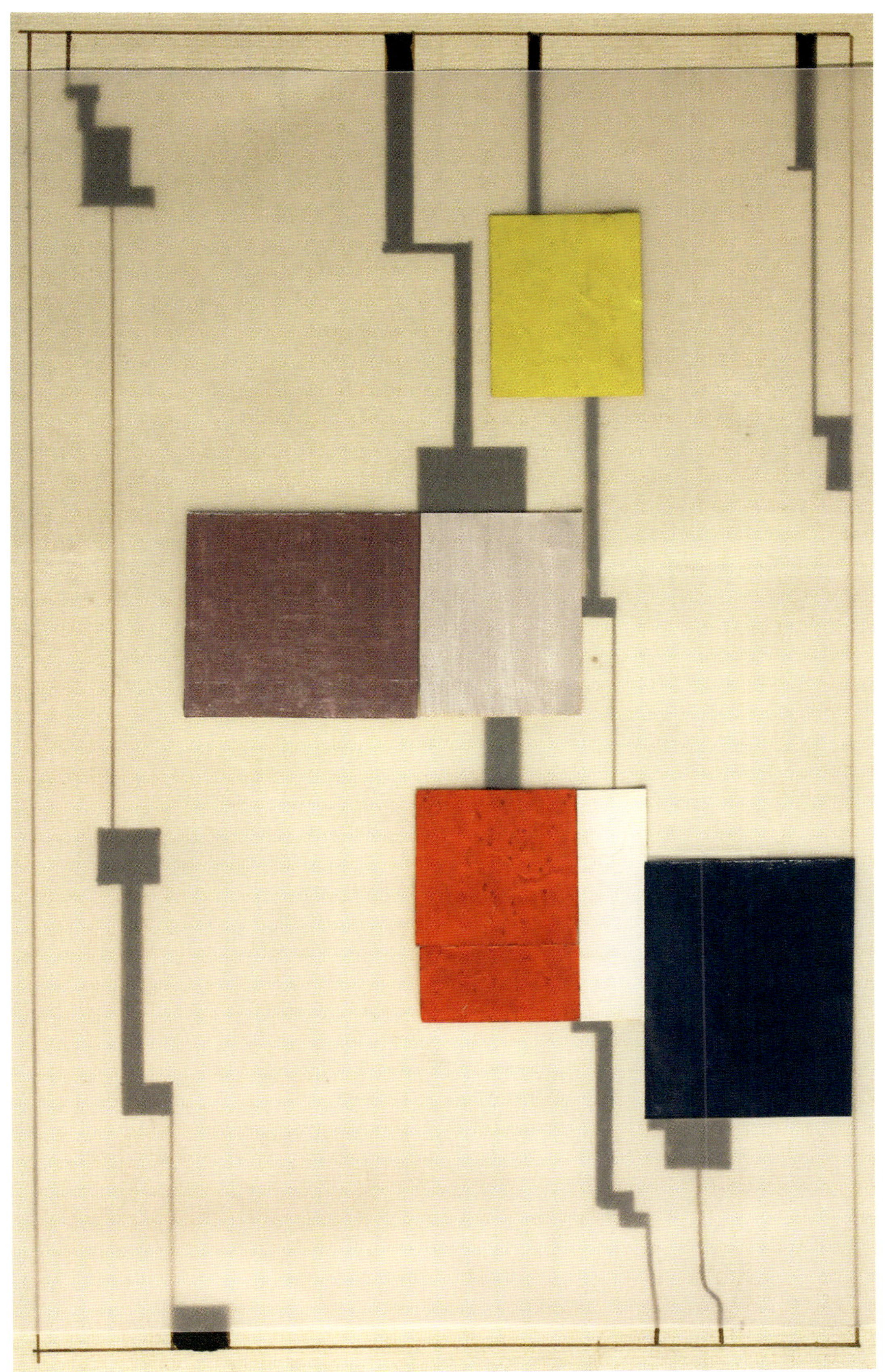

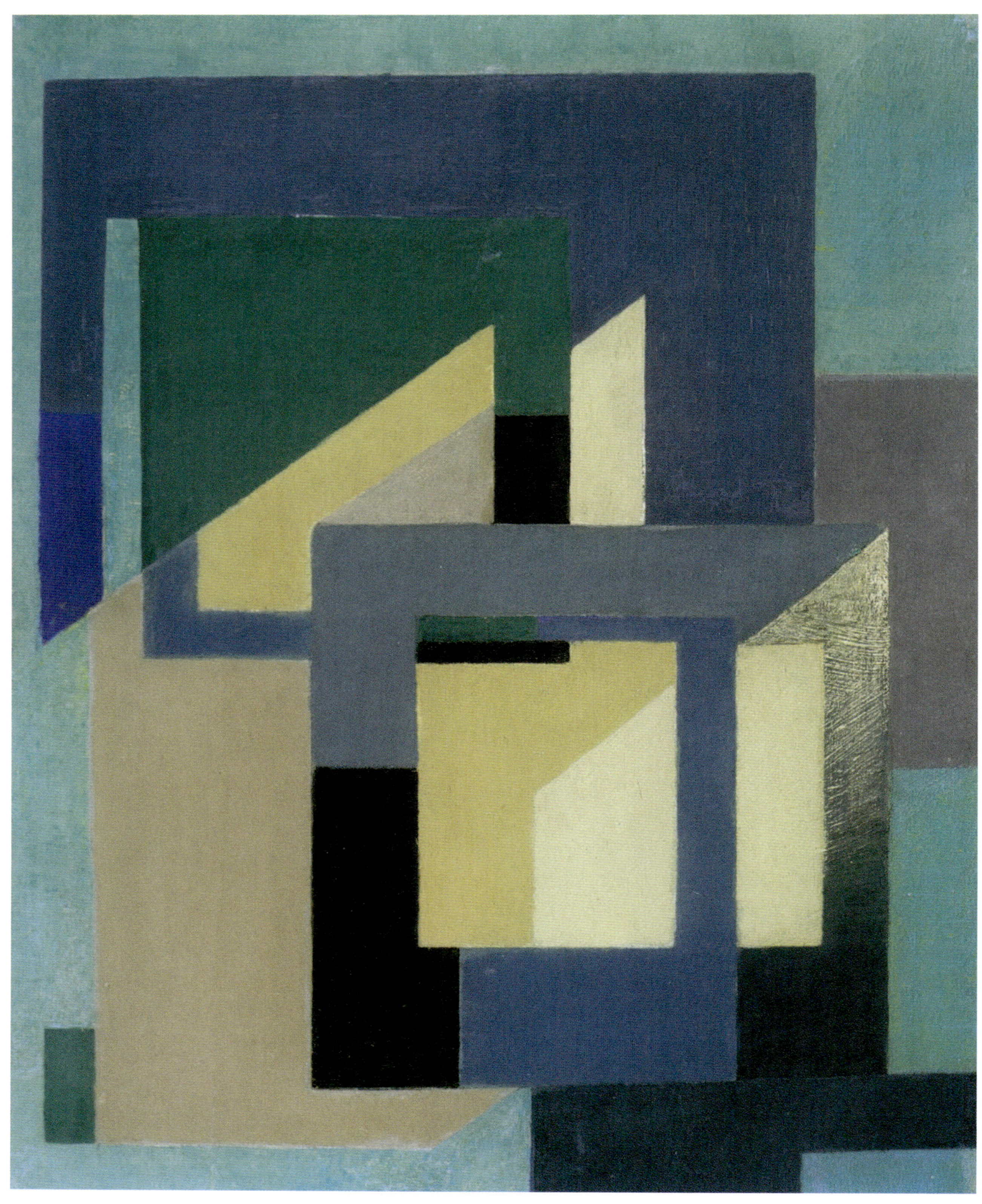

CAT. 10 — *Abstract*, c.1935, signed and inscribed verso,
oil on panel, 10 ½ × 8 ½ in. (26.5 × 21.5 cm).

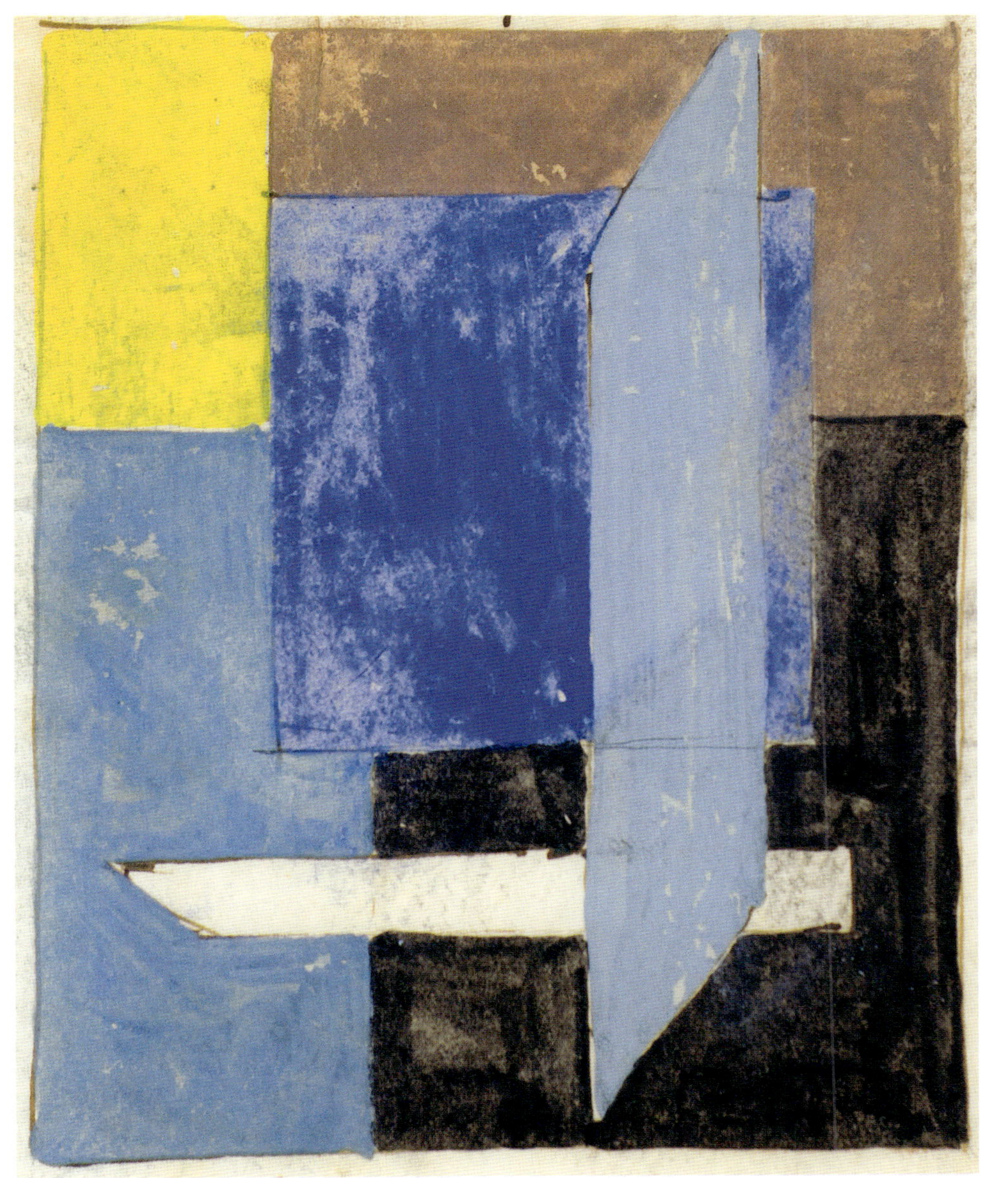

CAT. 11 — *Uprights, c. 1937, studio stamp to reverse,
gouache and pen & ink on paper,
4 x 3 ½ in. (10.5 x 8.9 cm).*

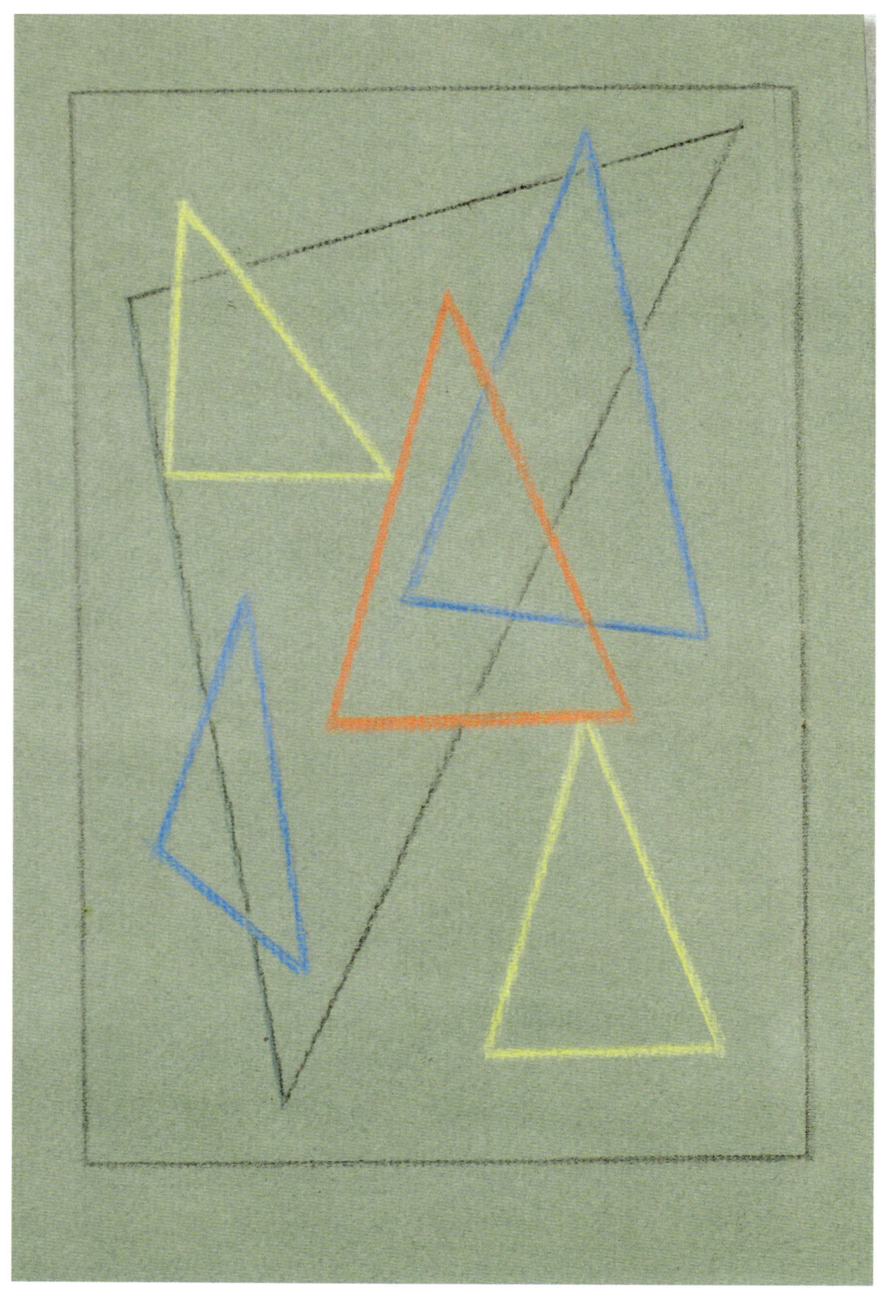

CAT. 12 – *Blue, Red and Yellow Triangles*, c.1938,
coloured pencil on grey/green paper, 8 x 5 ¼ in. (20.3 x 13.7 cm).
Provenance: The Artist's Estate; Private collection.

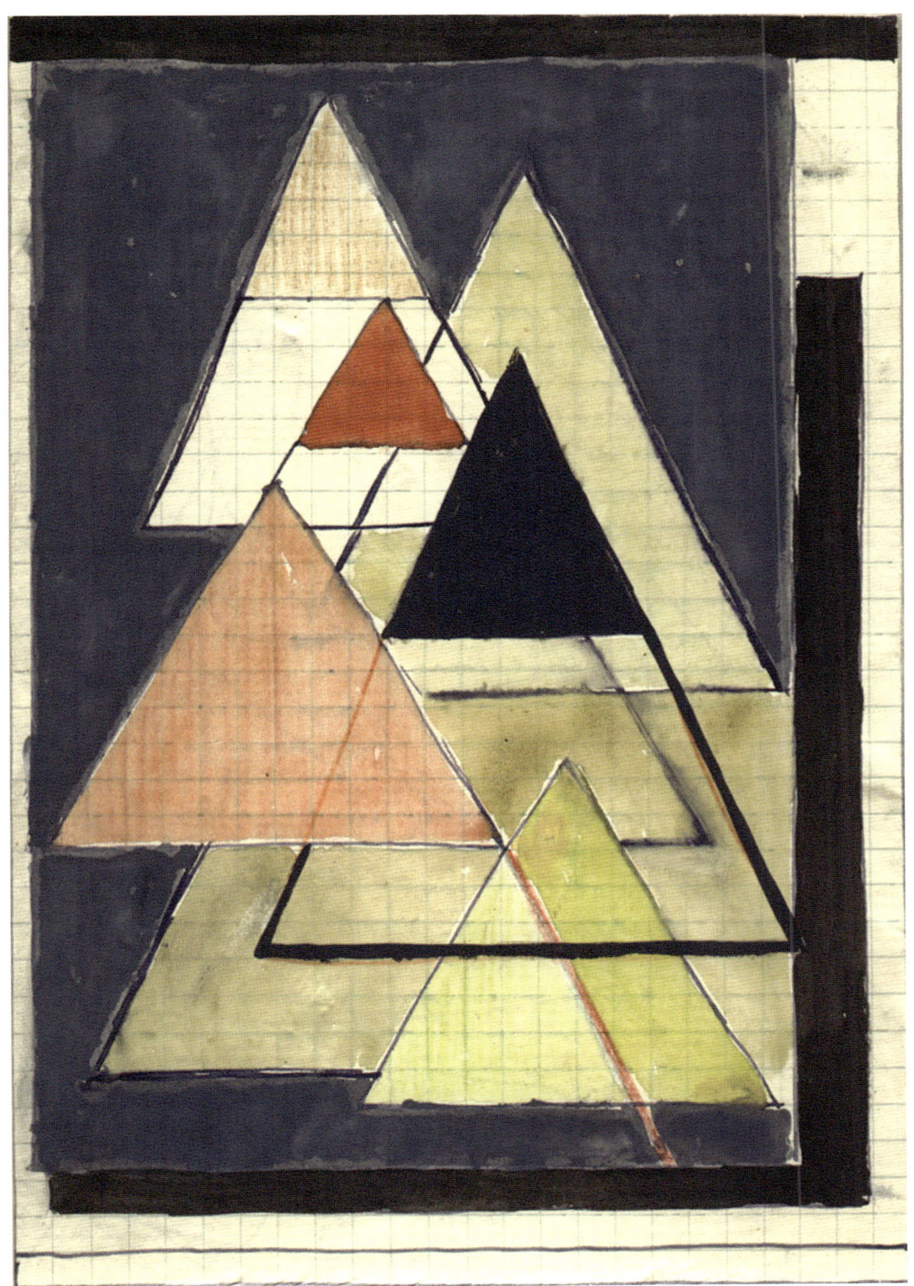

CAT. 13 – Sketch for *Triangle Series*, 1938/39,
coloured pencils on blue paper, 6 ¾ × 5 in. (17.2 × 12.7 cm).
Provenance: Marjorie Guthrie until c. 2000; Private collection.
Exhibited: *John Cecil Stephenson – Pioneer of Modernism*,
DLI Museum & Durham Art Gallery, 25 February - 29 April 2012.

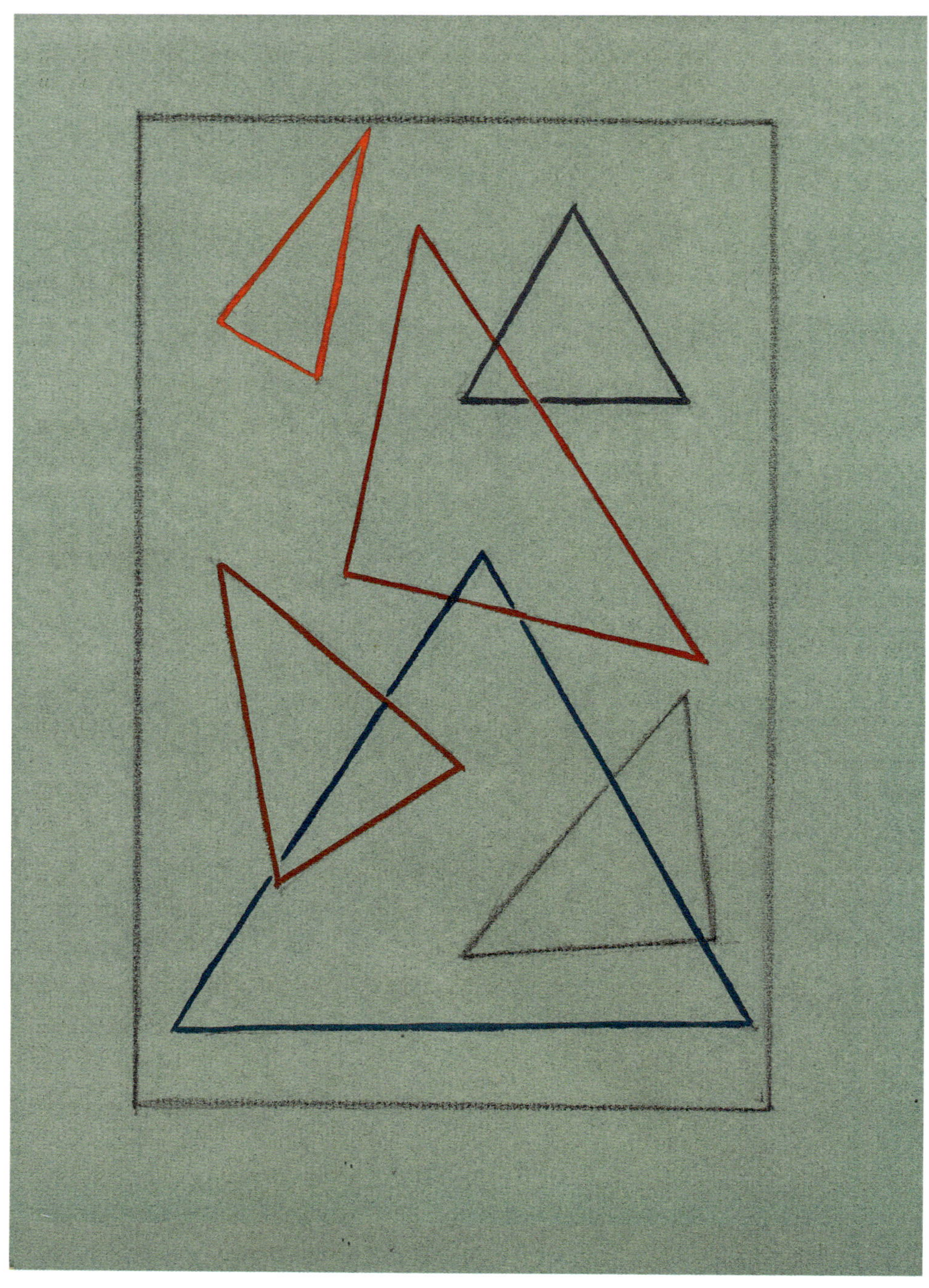

CAT. 14 – Sketch for *Triangle Series*, 1938/39,
coloured pencil on green paper, 9 ½ × 6 ¾ in. (24 × 17 cm).
Provenance: The Artist's Estate.
Literature: *John Cecil Stephenson*, Simon Guthrie, Cartmel Press, 1997, p. 148.

CAT. 15 – *Orange Sketch*, 1939, signed with studio stamp to reverse,
gouache on paper, squared and inscribed with measurements, 7 ¼ × 5 ¼ in. (18.4 × 13.3 cm).
Provenance: Marjorie Guthrie until c. 2000; Private collection.
Exhibited: *John Cecil Stephenson – Pioneer of Modernism*, DLI Museum & Durham Art Gallery,
25 February - 29 April 2012.

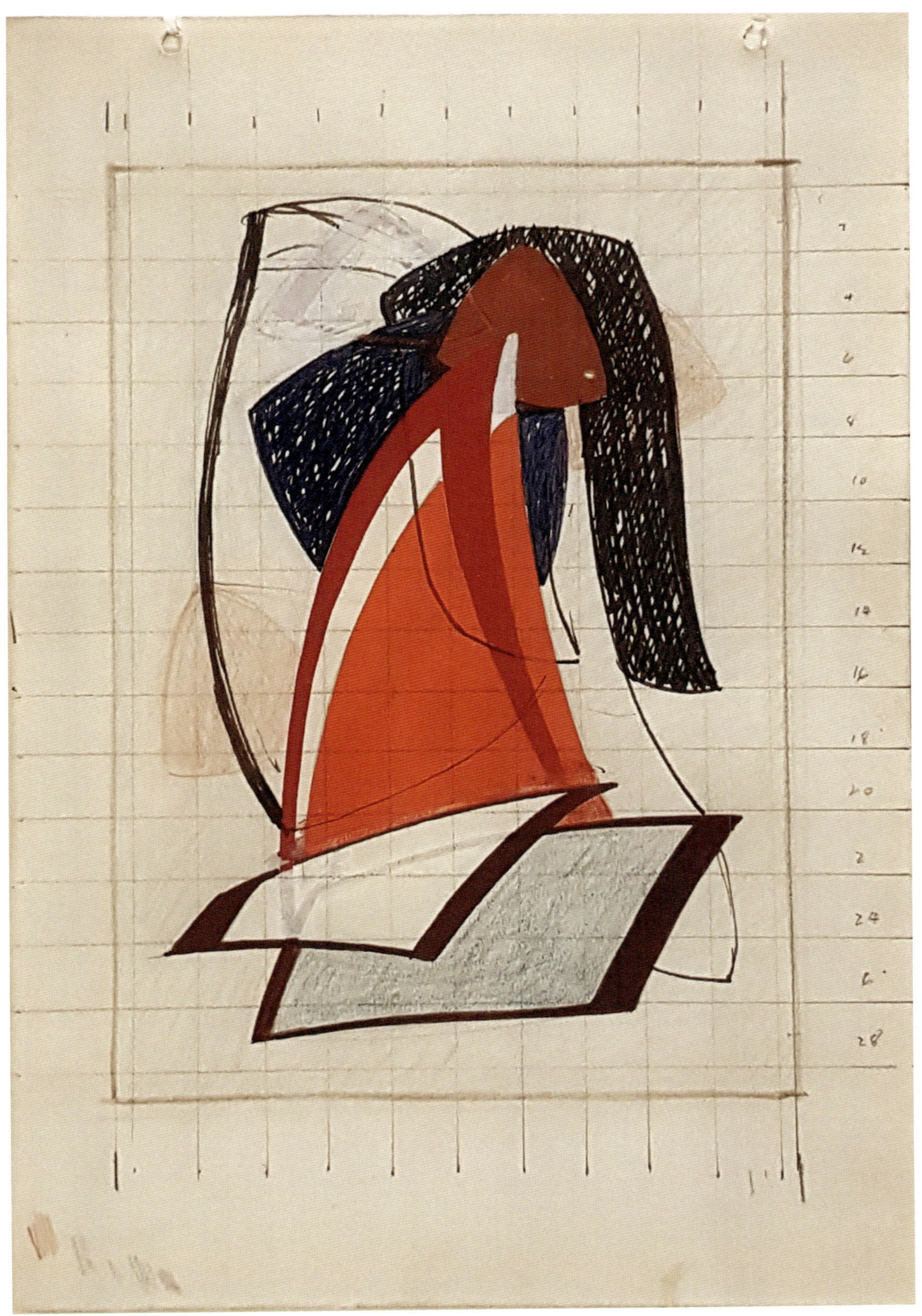

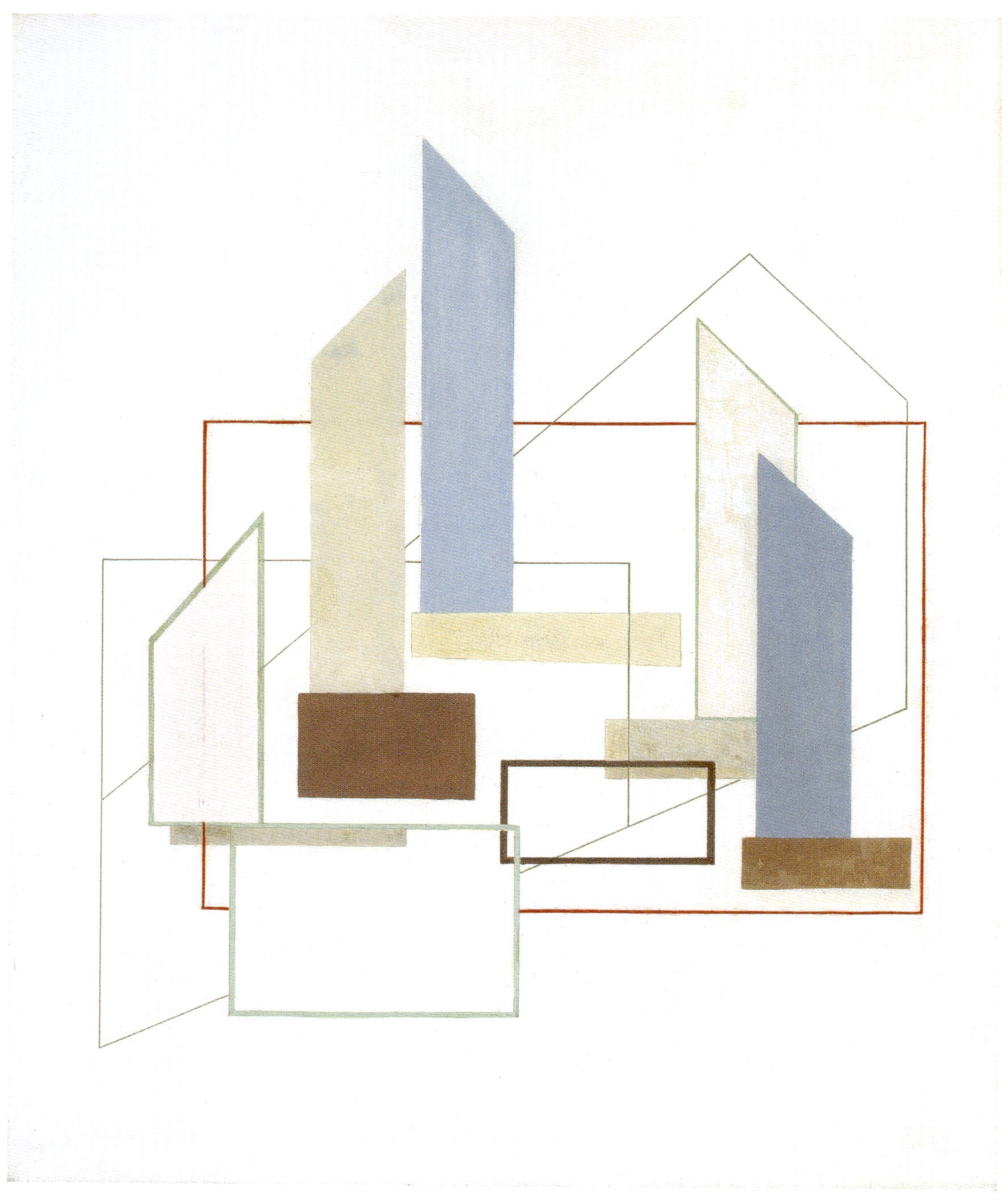

CAT. 16 – *Rust, Indigo, Blue, Buff,* 1937, signed and inscribed verso,
gouache on paper, 21 ¾ × 17 ½ inches (26.5 × 21.5 cm).
Exhibited: The Fine Art Society, 2007.

CAT. 17 – *Vortex I,* 1939, signed verso,
egg tempera on canvas, 26 × 20 in. (66 × 51 cm).
Exhibited: Camden Arts Centre, 1975; Fischer Fine Art, 1976.
Literature: Simon Guthrie, *John Cecil Stephenson,* 1997, (12) illustrated p. 138.

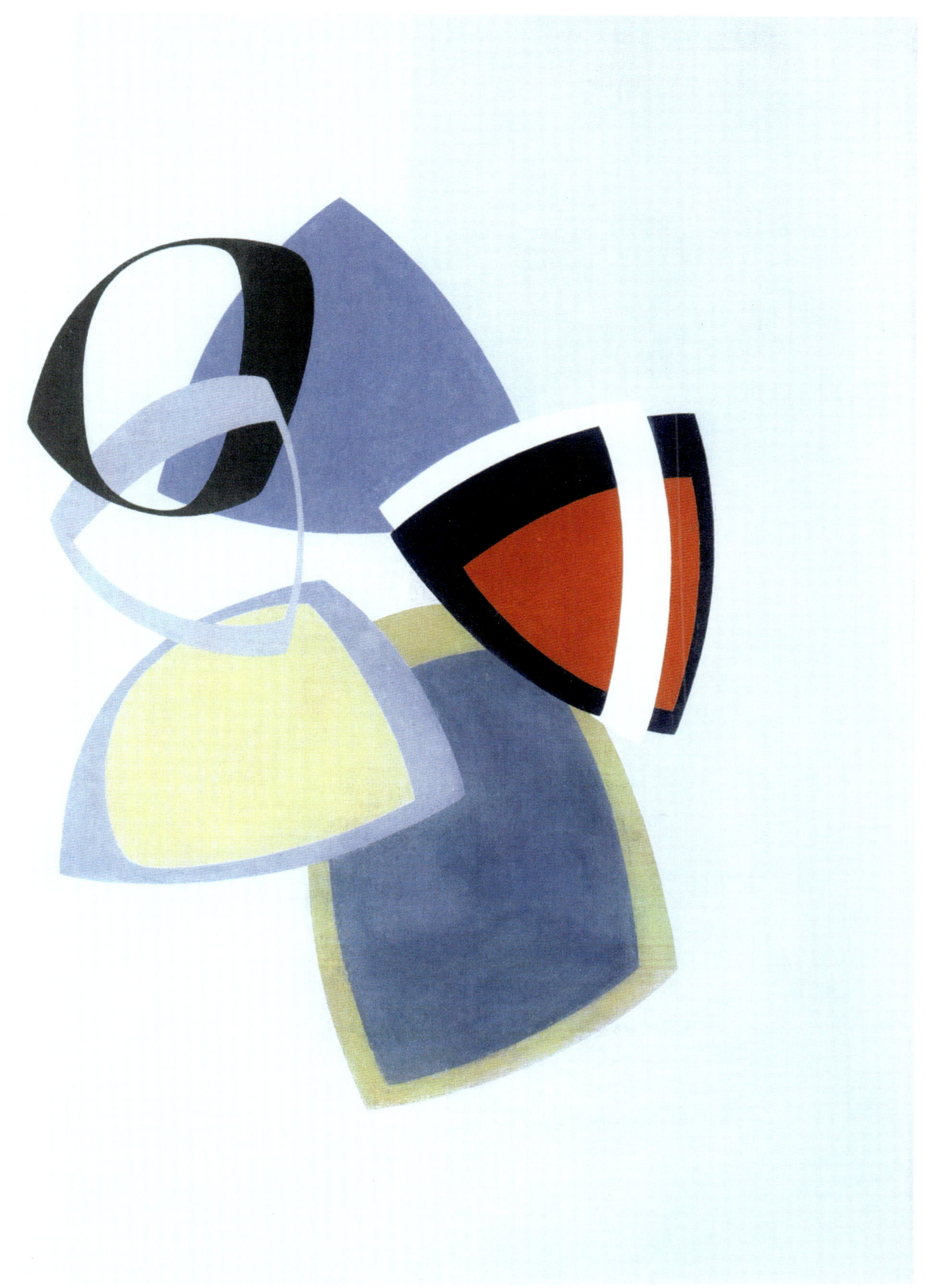

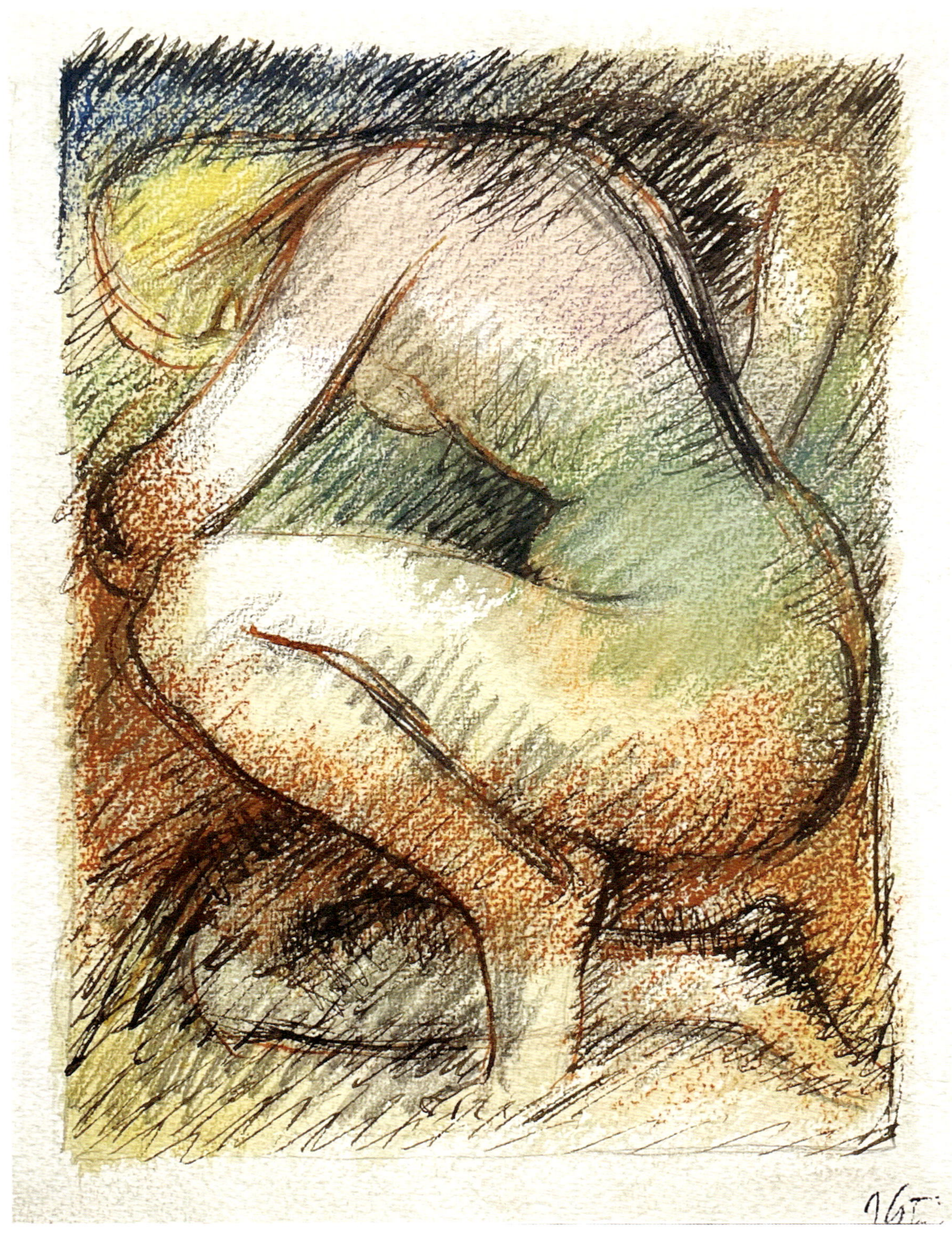

CAT. 18– *Kneeling nude*, c.1940, signed twice with studio stamp,
colour chalk and pastel over and pen & ink on paper, 11 x 11 in. (26 x 26 cm).
Provenance: The Artist's family; Private collection.

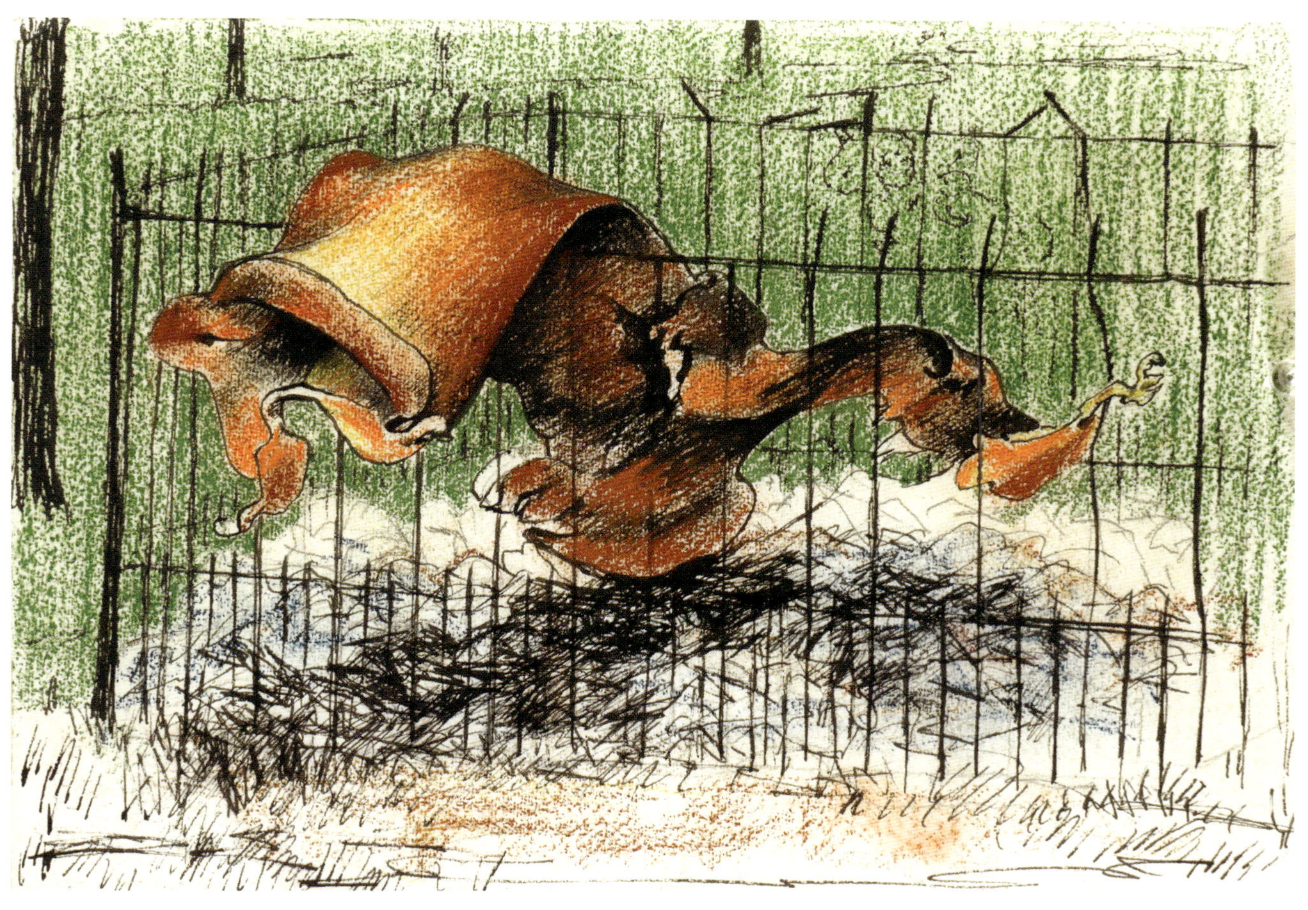

CAT. 19 — *The End of a Doodlebug, Hampstead Heath, 1945,*
signed and dated, Inscribed by the artist on the reverse in pen and ink: 'End of a Doodlebug Hampstead Heath.
chalk and pastel over pencil and pen & ink on paper, 10 × 14 in. (25.5 × 35.5 cm).
Provenance: The Artist's family.
Exhibited: WW2 - War Pictures by British Artists, Morley College London, 28 October -23 November 2016.
Literature: *WW2 — War Pictures by British Artists*, Edited by Sacha Llewellyn & Paul Liss, July 2016, cat 39, page 77.

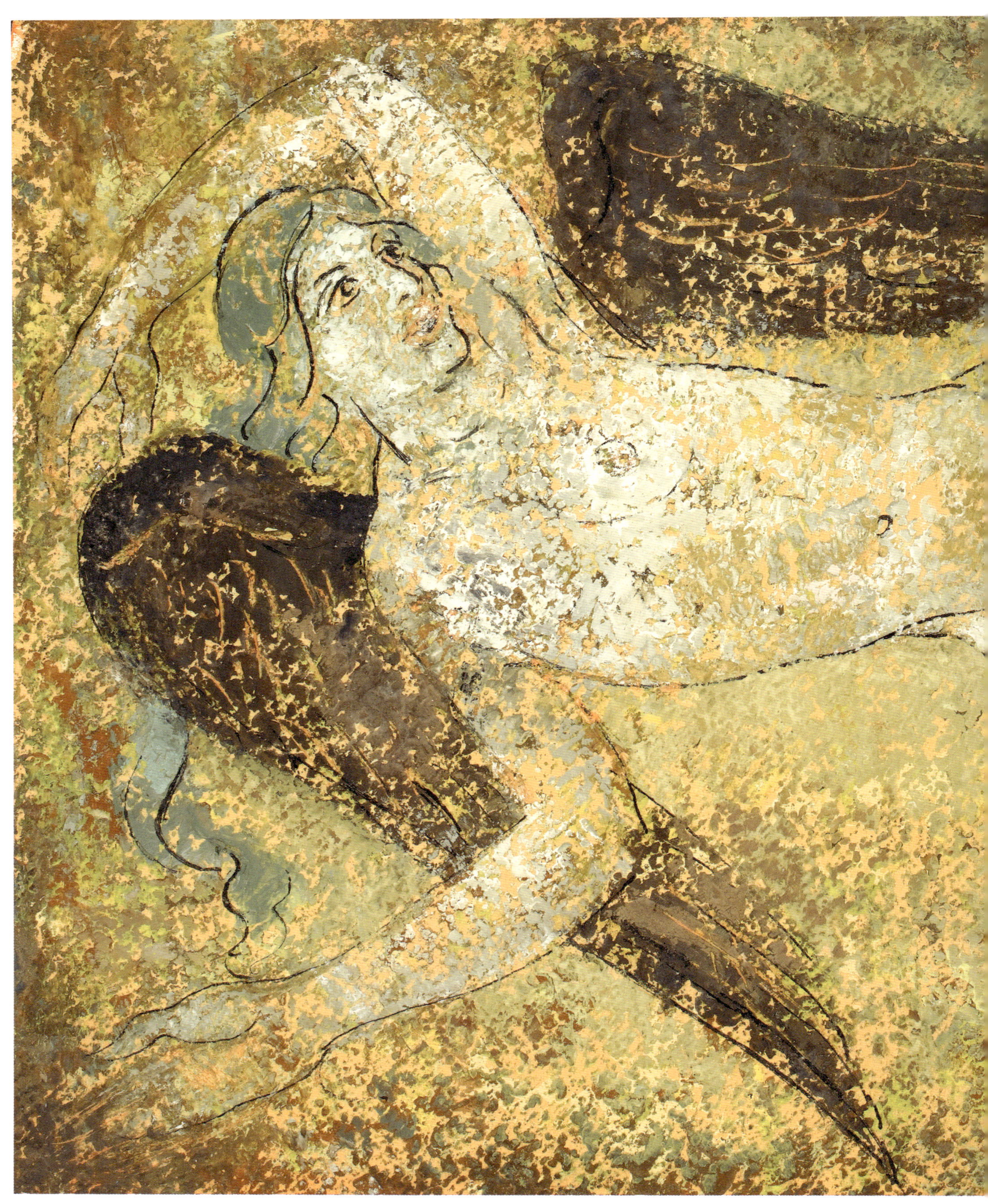

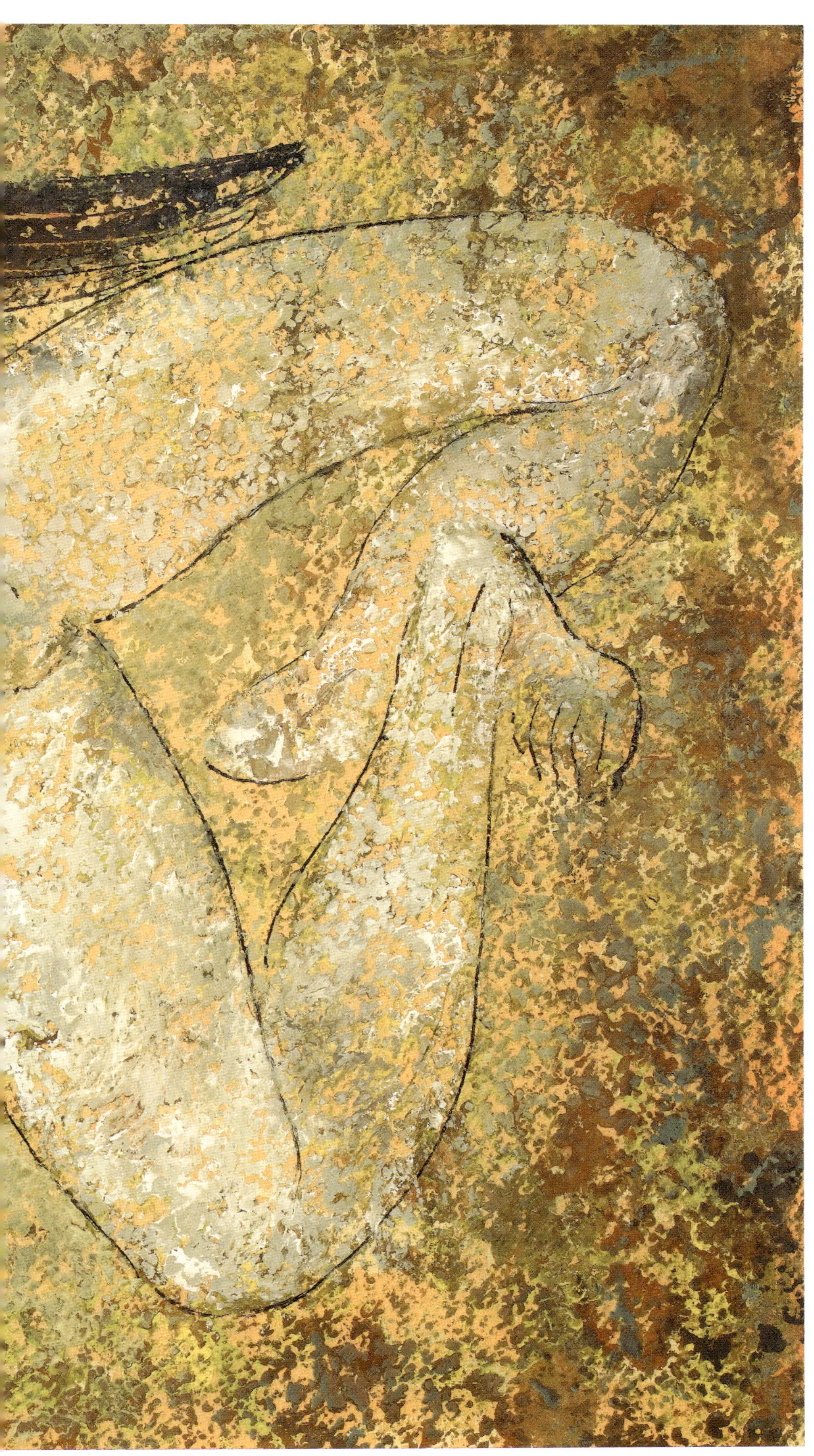

CAT. 20– *Perseus and Andromeda*, 1945,
signed, dated and inscribed
with title on reverse,
oil on card, 16 × 22 ½ (40.5 × 57 cm).
Provenance: Marjorie Guthrie;
Private collection.

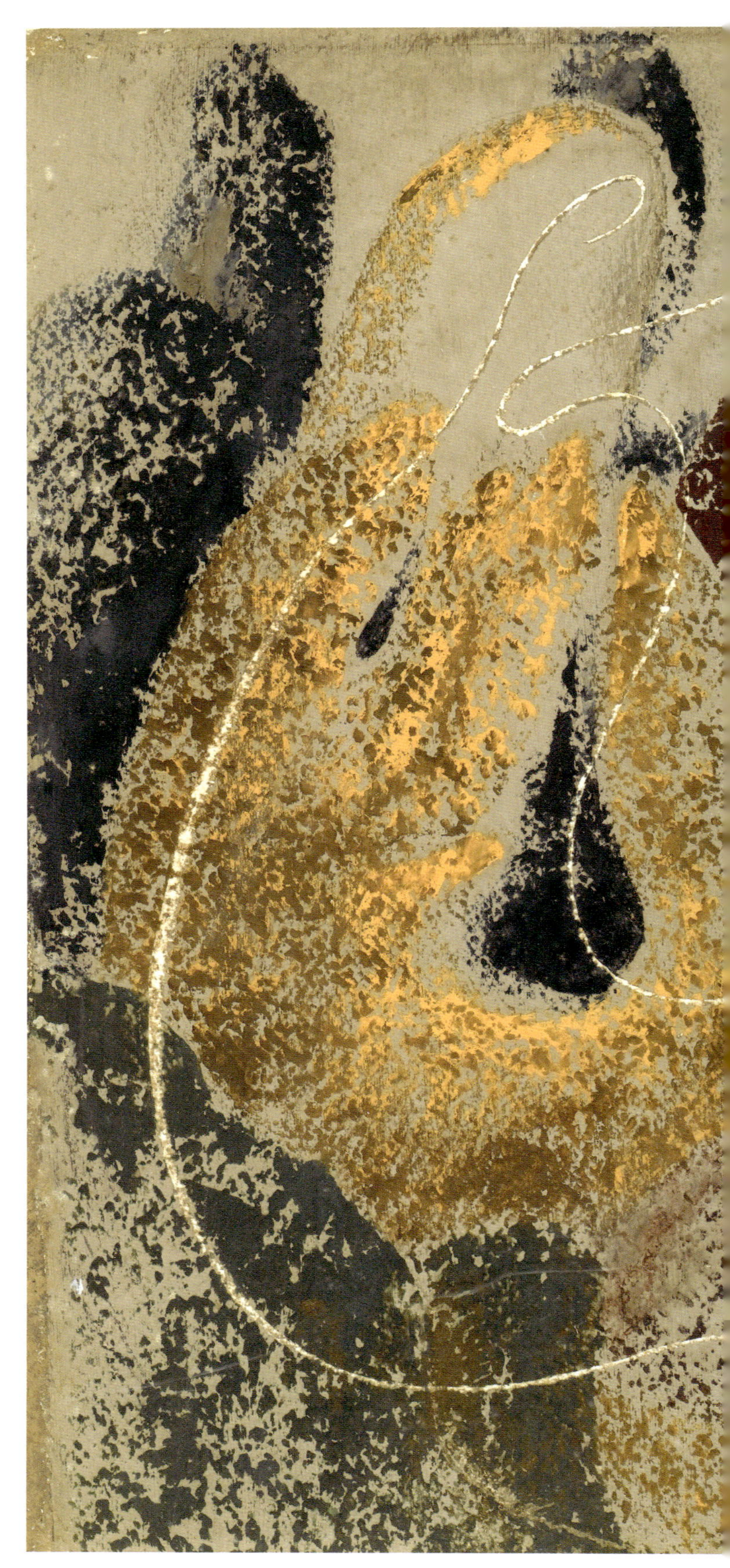

CAT. 21 – *Madonna of the Rocks*, 1945,
signed with initials, signed, dated and inscribed on the reverse,
oil on paper with scratching out, 16 × 21 in. (40.7 × 53.3 cm).
Provenance: The Artist's family.

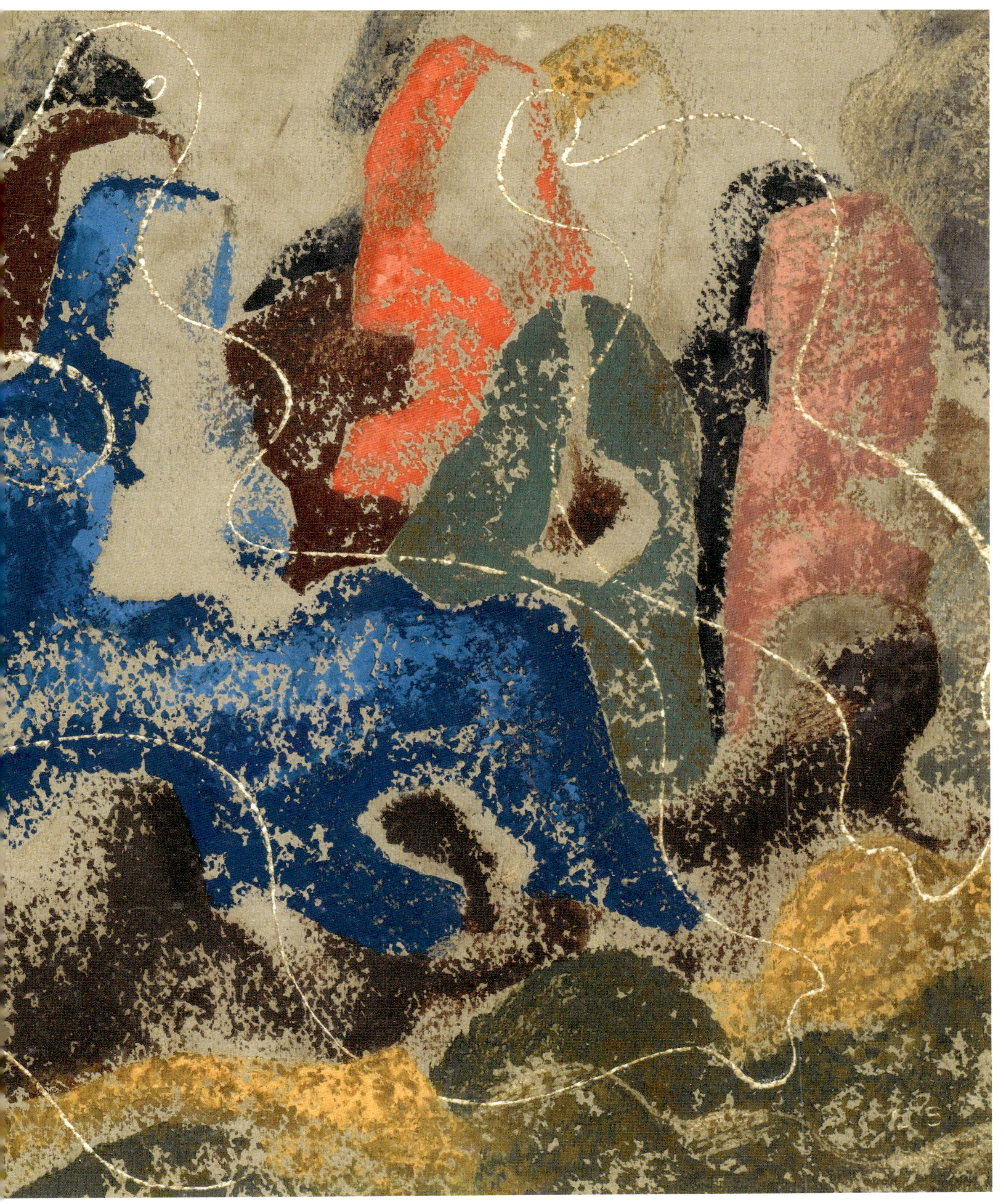

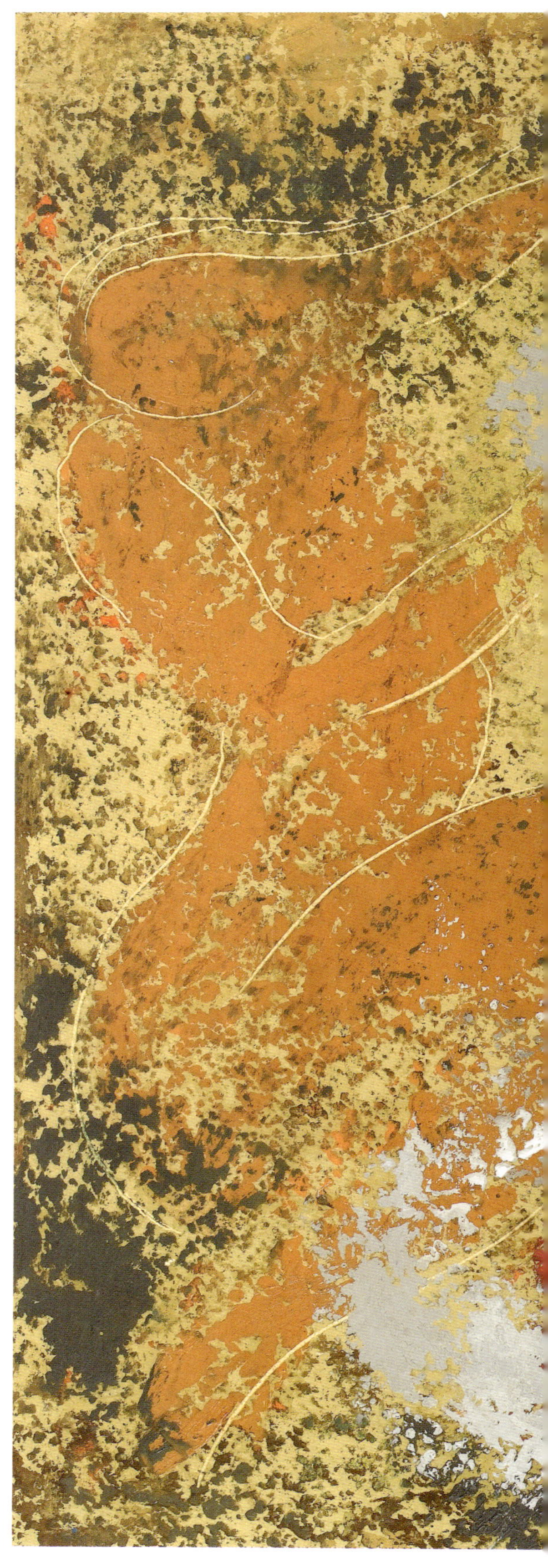

CAT. 22 – *Three Graces*, 1945, signed and titled on the reverse,
oil on prepared paper with scratching out, 18 × 22 ½ in. (45.7 × 57.1 cm).
Provenance: The Artist's family.

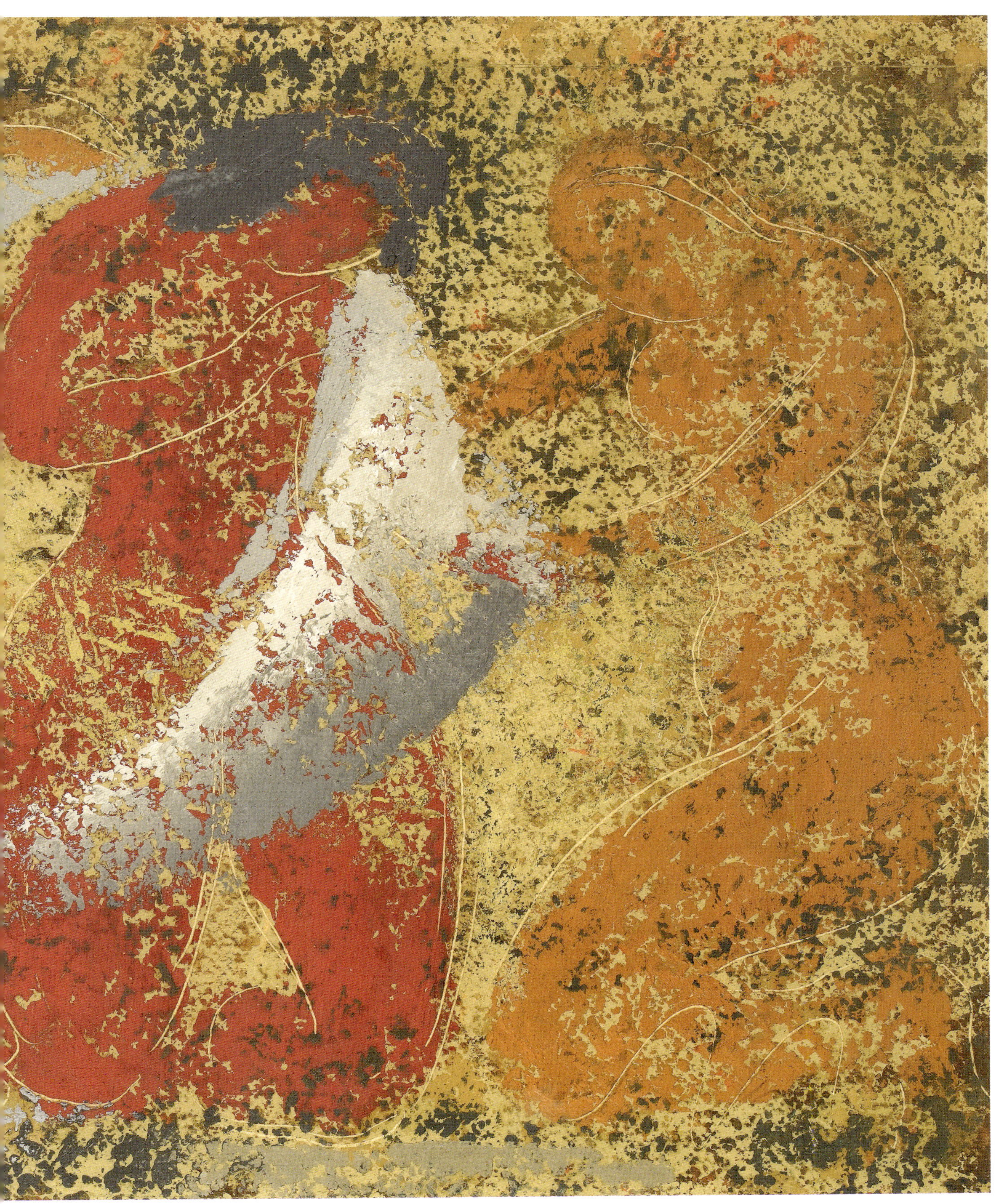

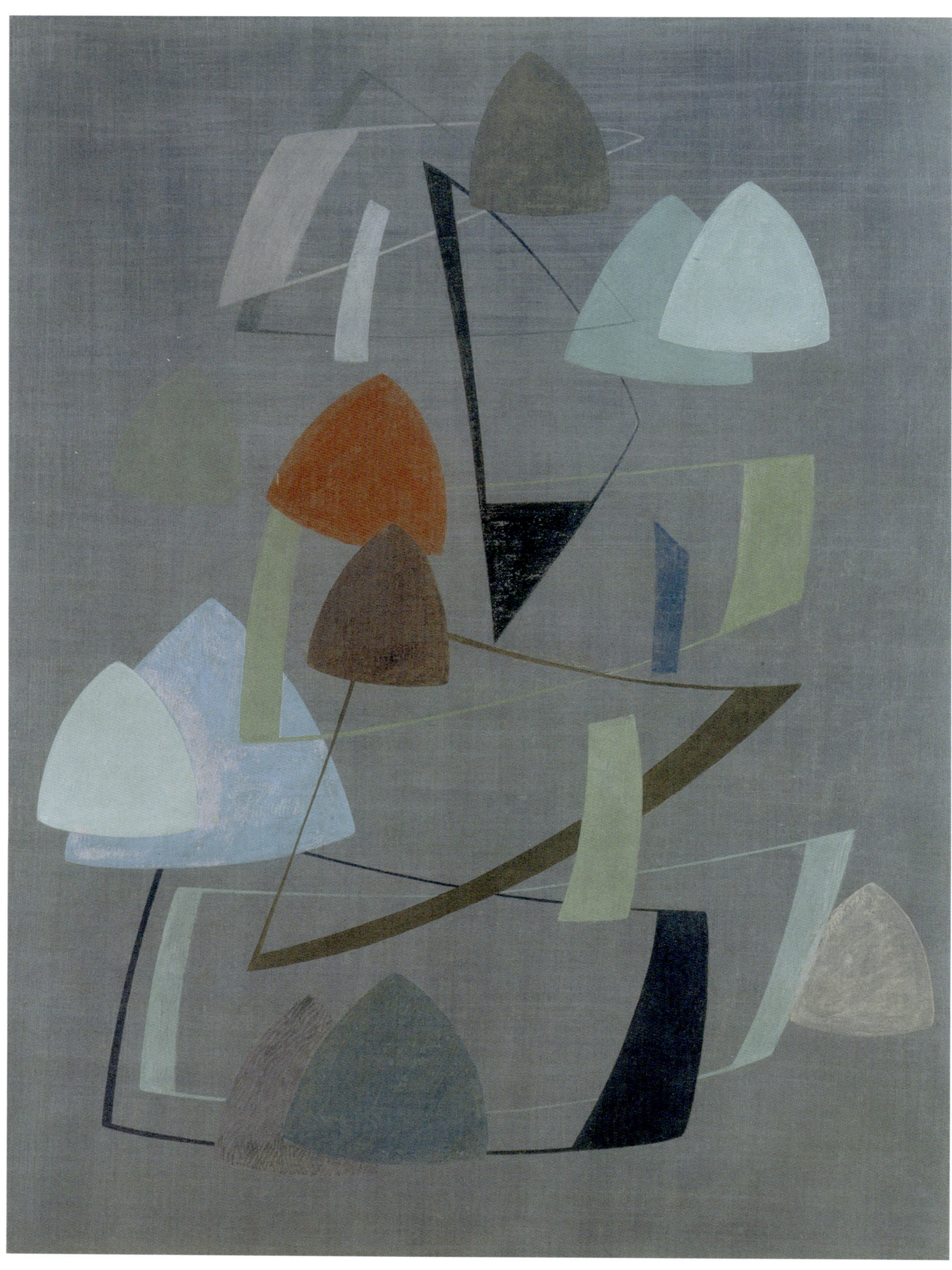

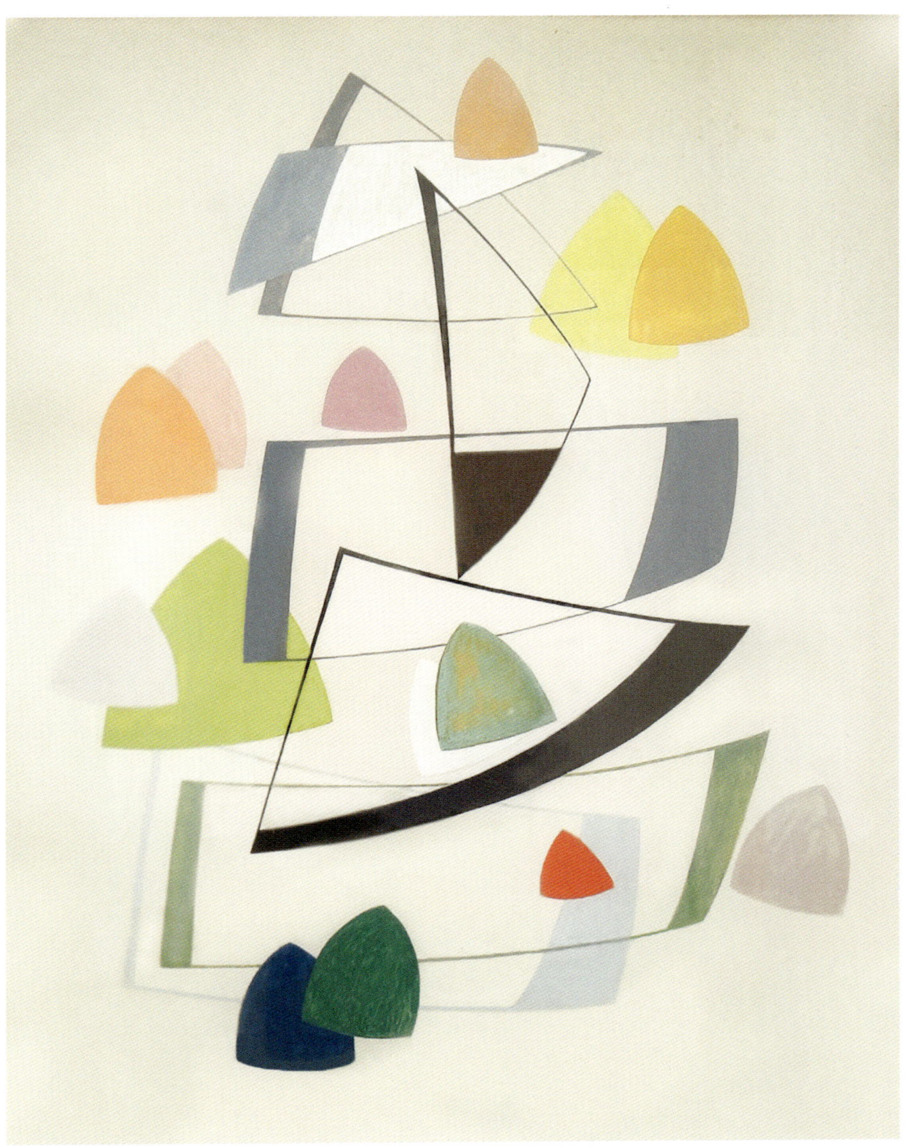

CAT. 24 – *Divertimento II*, 1955,
egg tempera on board, 29 x 22 in. (73.5 x 56 cm). Collection: Tony Mould.

CAT. 23 – *Clarabella*, 1950, signed verso,
tempera on board, 32 x 24 in. (81.3 x 61 cm).
Provenance: The artist, and by descent. Their sale; Phillips, London, 17 November 1998, lot 83. Peter Nahum. with Galeria Milano, Milan. His sale; Christie's, London, 15 November 2006, lot 290. 2007-2020: Private collection.
Exhibition: London, Fischer Fine Art, *Cecil Stephenson 1889-1965*, October - November 1976, no. 16, as 'Painting'. London, Fine Art Society, *John Cecil Stephenson*, October - November 2007, no. 14.
Literature: *John Cecil Stephenson*, Simon Guthrie, 1997; *John Cecil Stephenson*, The Fine Art Society in association with Paul Liss, catalogue number 14; *John Cecil Stephenson – Pioneer of Modernism*, Conor Mullan, DLI Museum and Art Gallery, 2012.

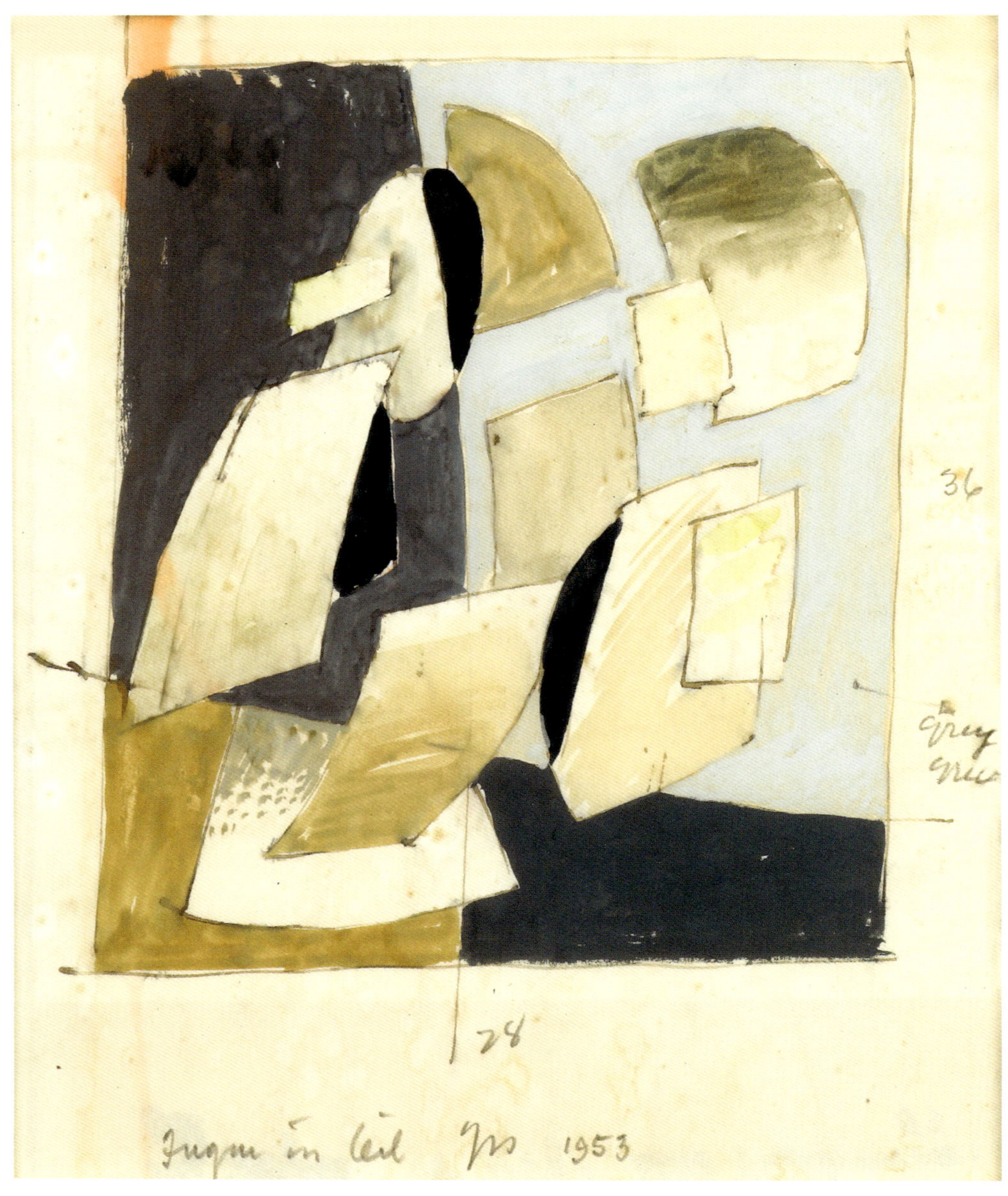

CAT. 25 — Study for *Fugue*, 1953, titled and inscribed in pencil,
gouache and indian ink on paper, 10 x 7 ½ in. (25.4 x 19 cm).
Exhibited: *John Cecil Stephenson — Pioneer of Modernism*,
DLI Museum & Durham Art Gallery, 25 February - 29 April 2012.

CAT. 26 — *Rondo* (Subtitled "a nous la liberte"), 1953,
gouache on paper, 7 ¾ x 5 ¾ in. (19.5 x 14.6 cm).
Provenance: Marjorie Guthrie until c.2000; Private collection.
Exhibited: *John Cecil Stephenson — Pioneer of Modernism*,
DLI Museum & Durham Art Gallery, 25 February - 29 April 2012.

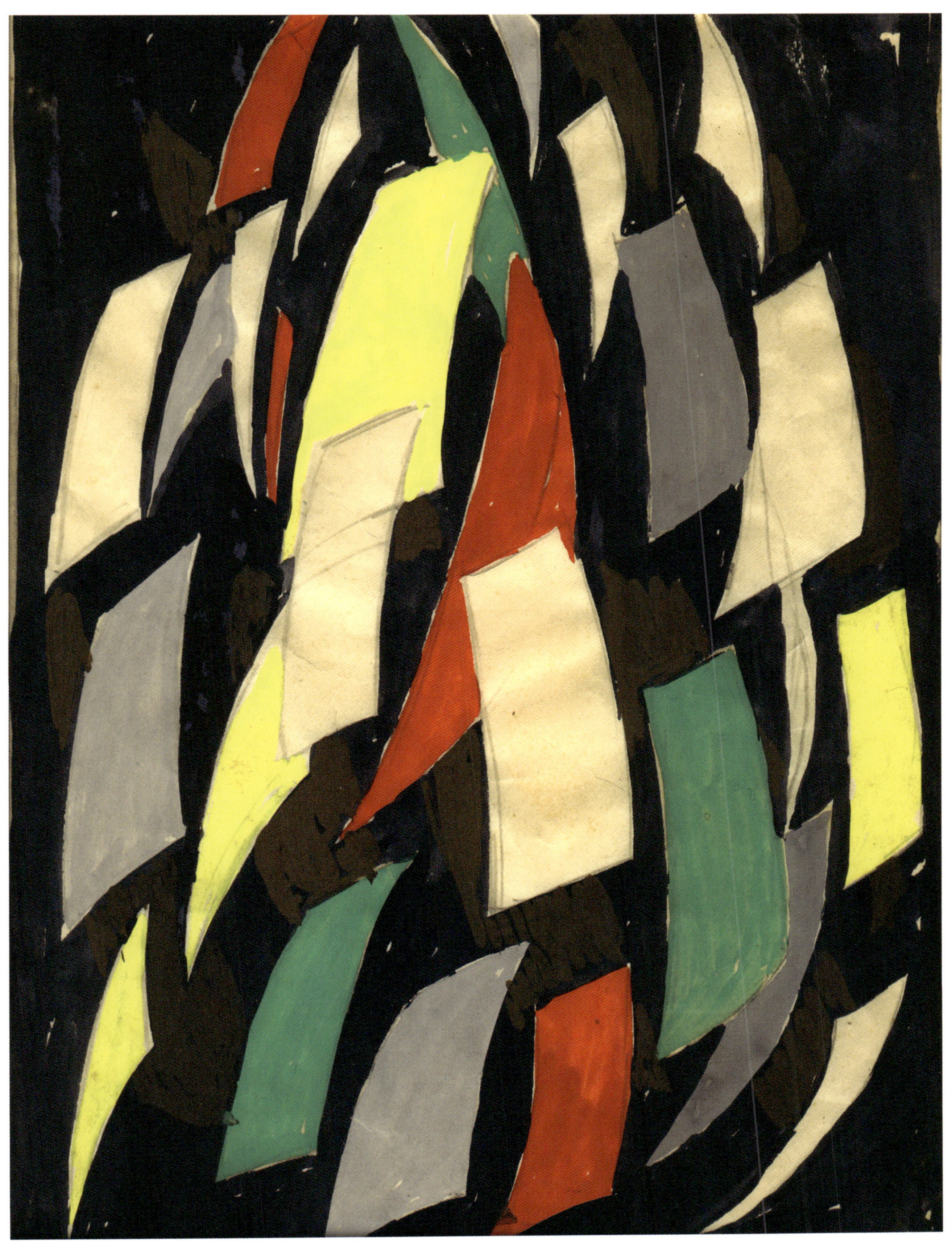

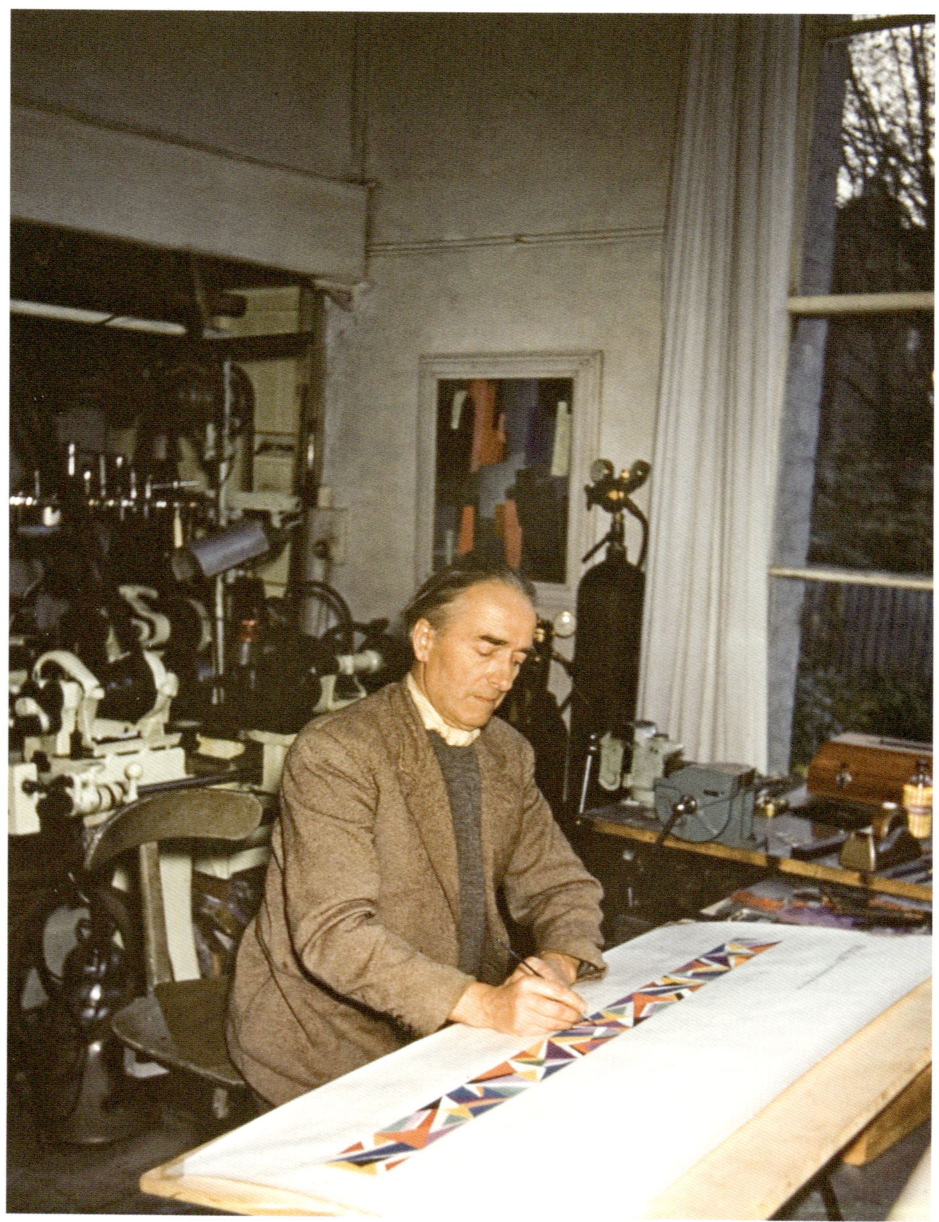

Fig. 29 – Stephenson working on the *Plyglass* design for facia panel of the 1958 Brussels Exhibition. *Tonality* (**CAT. 27**) can be seen hanging behind him; it remained in his studio until his death a decade later.

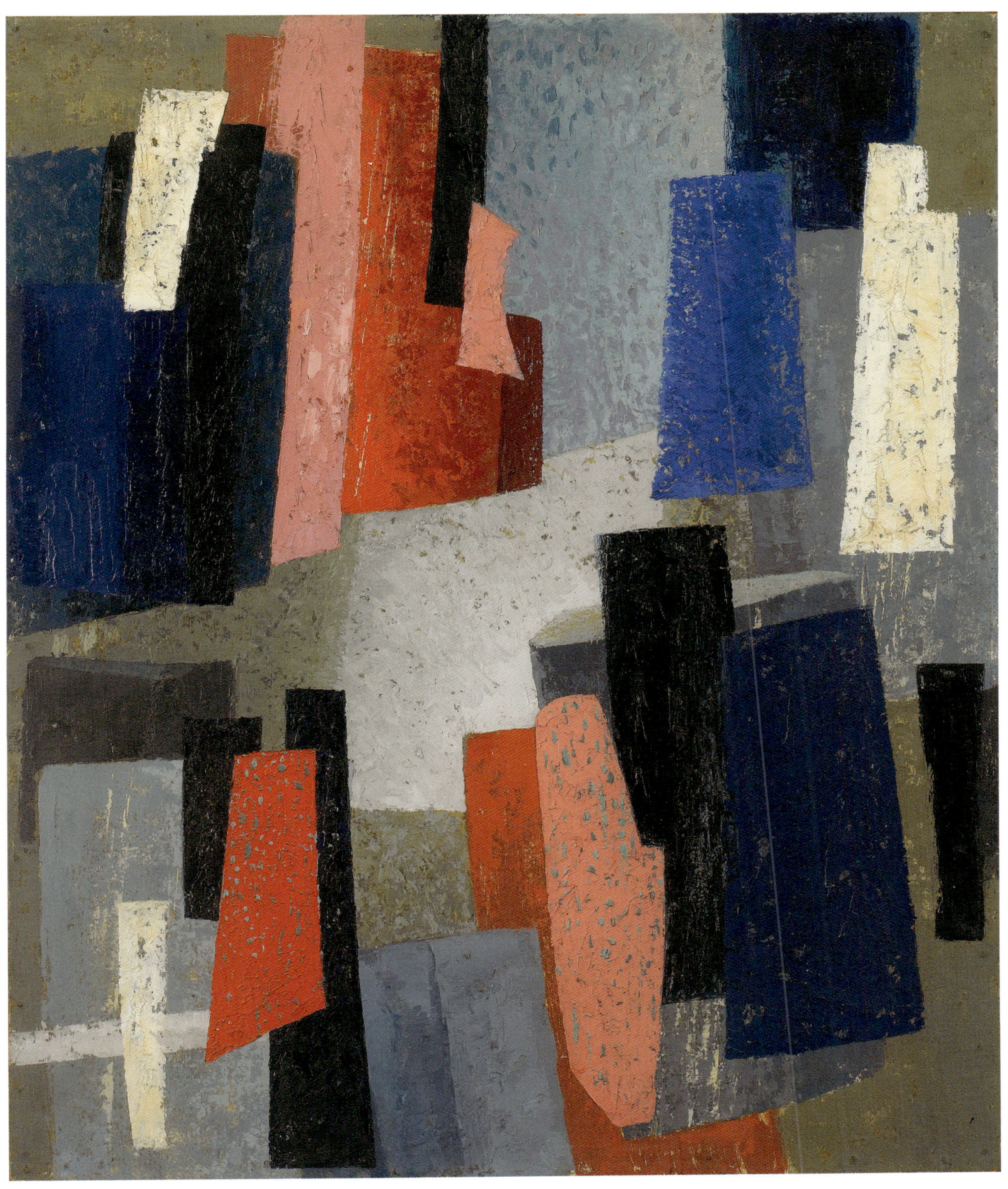

CAT. 27 – *Tonality*, 1954, signed, titled and dated on reverse
oil on canvas, 24 × 20 in. (61 × 51 cm).

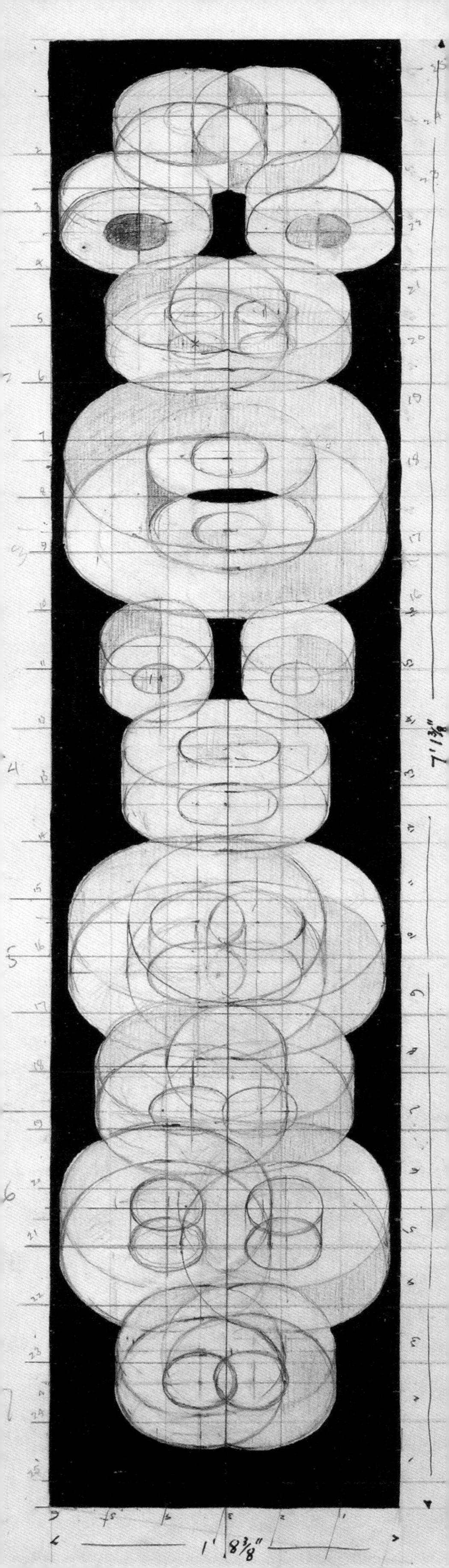

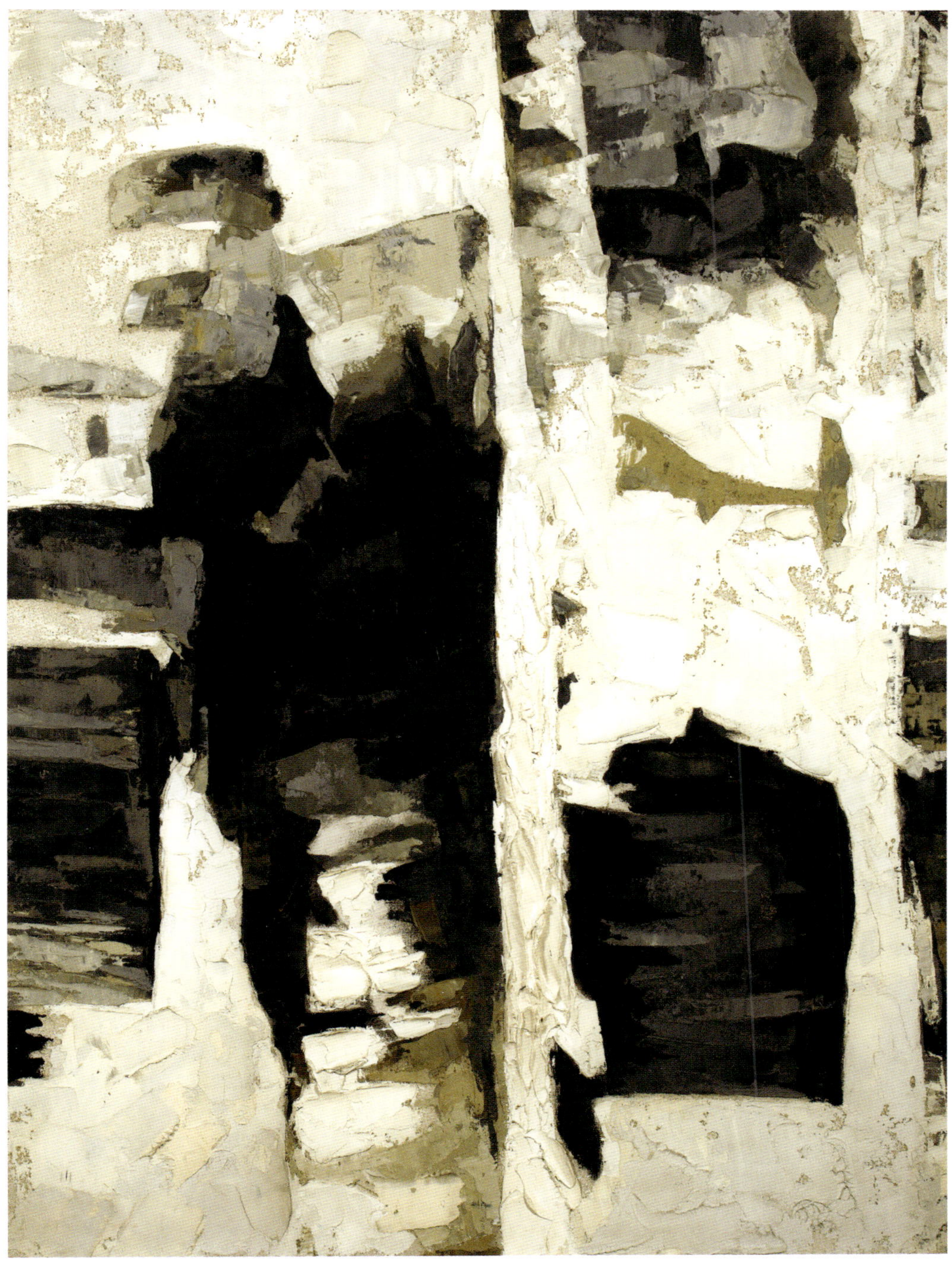

CAT. 29 – *Monody*, 1960, signed and titled on the reverse; labelled to the reverse, "not for sale",
oil on board, 48 × 36 in. (122 × 91.5 cm). Provenance: Marjorie Guthrie.
Exhibited: Drian Gallery, September 1960, no 3; *Cecil Stephenson, A Retrospective Exhibition*, 29 January-19
February 1975, Camden Arts Centre, no. 70.
Literature: Simon Guthrie, *John Cecil Stephenson*, 1997, p. 119, ill. p. 150.

CAT. 28 – Preliminary study for plyglass mural, Queen Mary's College, 1957, signed, inscribed with title and dated in pen & ink,
gouache, crayon and pencil, squared, 21 ¼ × 6 ¼ in. (54 × 16 cm).
Provenance: Marjorie Guthrie.

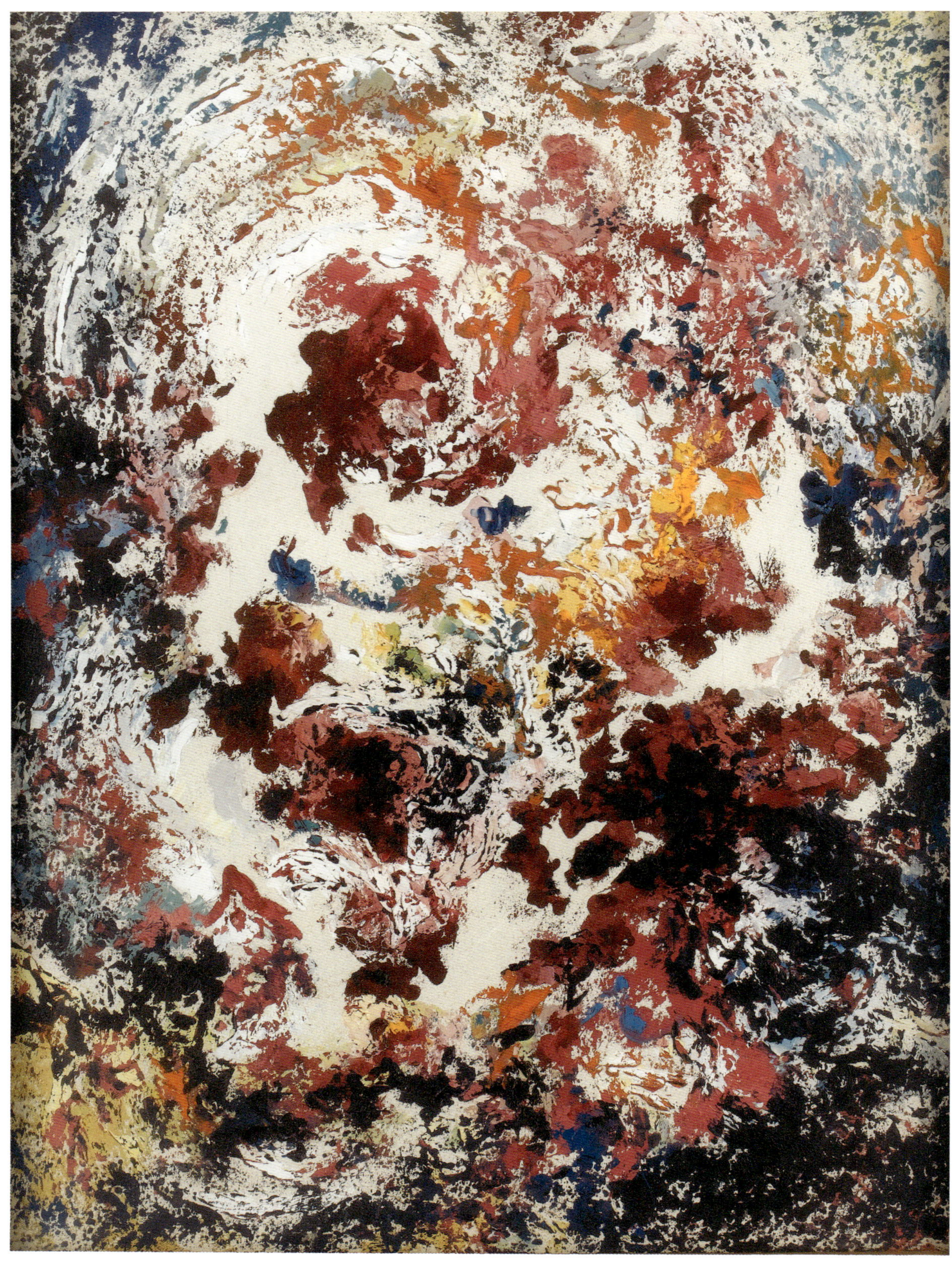

CAT. 30 — *Tita*, c.1960, titled on reverse,
oil on prepared a board, 30 × 22 in. (76 × 56 cm).
Provenance: Marjorie Guthrie.

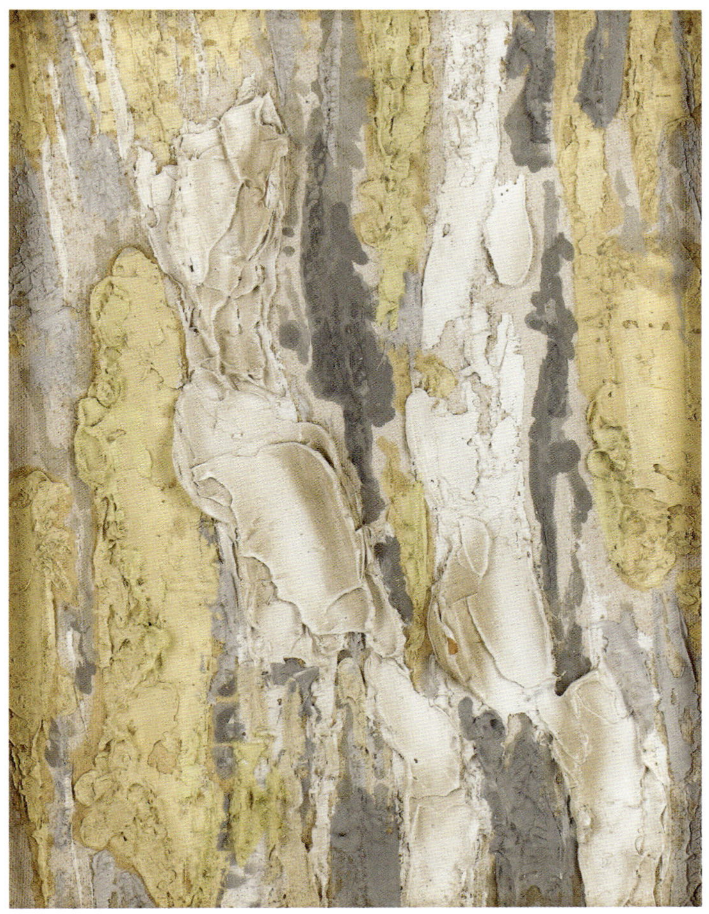

CAT. 31 – *Carpriccioso*, c.1959, signed and dated on the reverse,
oil on board, 11 ¾ × 9 in. (30 × 23 cm).
Provenance: Marjorie Guthrie.

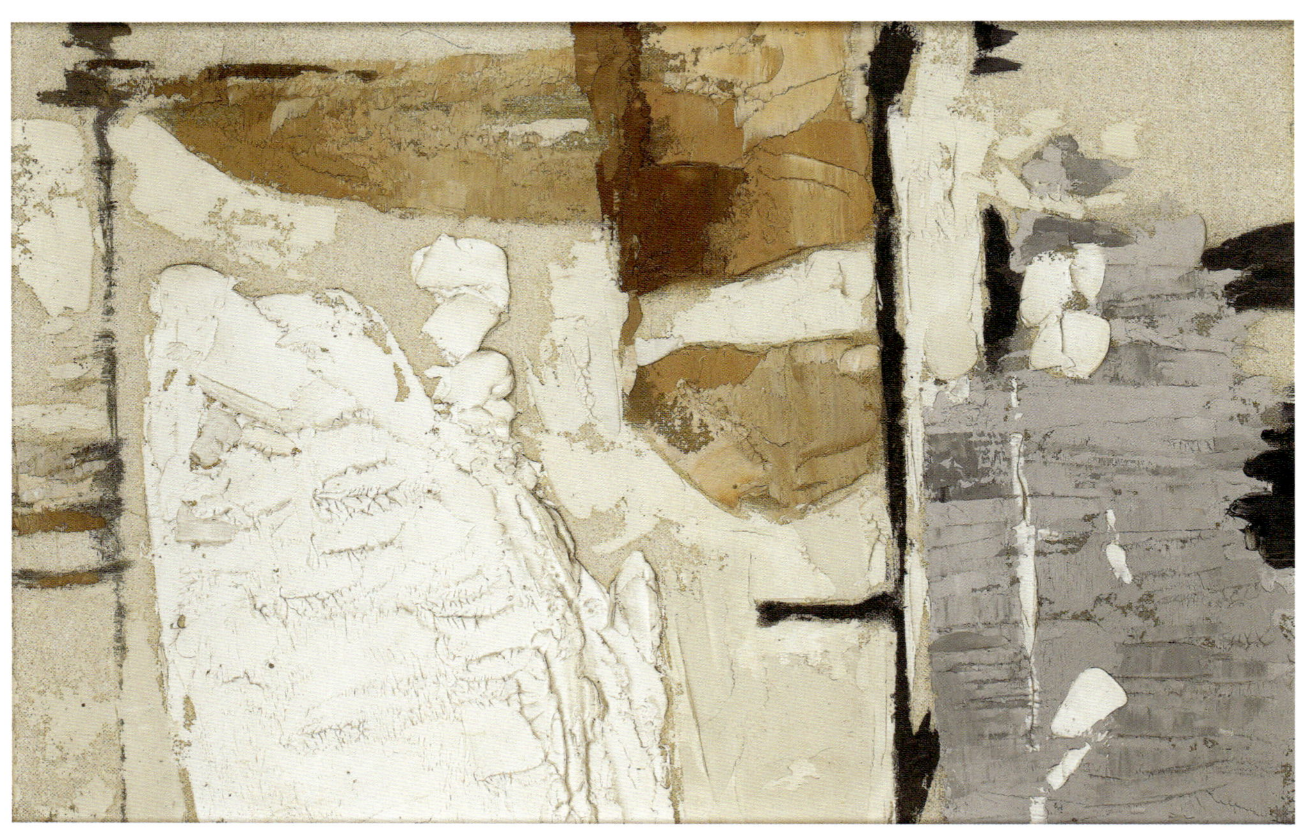

CAT. 32 — *Accent*, 1960, signed, dated and titled on the reverse,
oil on board, 15 x 22 in. (38.1 x 55.9 cm).
Provenance: The Artist's family.
Exhibited: Drian Gallery Stephenson, September 1960, CAT 13.

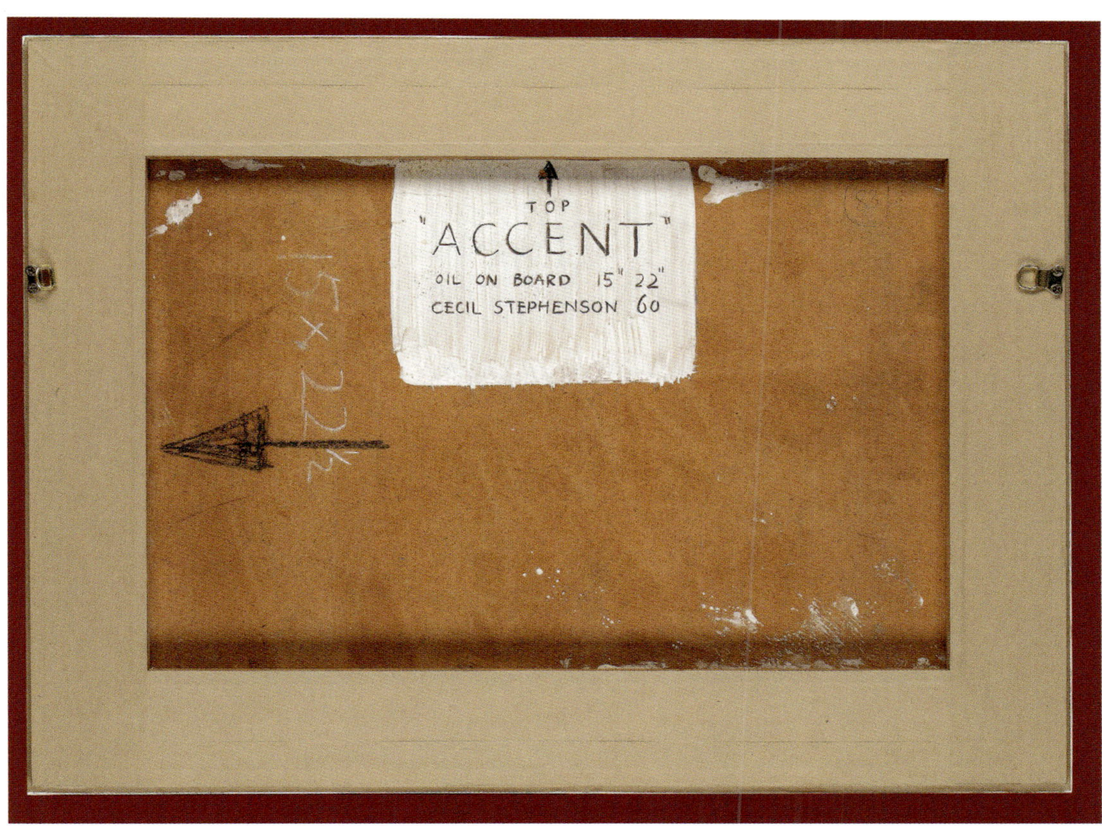

Fig. 30 – *Reverse of Accent.*

Pages 86-87: **CAT. 33** – *Abnegation*, 1960, signed, titled and dated to reverse,
oil on canvas, 15 × 24 in. (38 × 61 cm).
Provenance: Marjorie Guthrie.

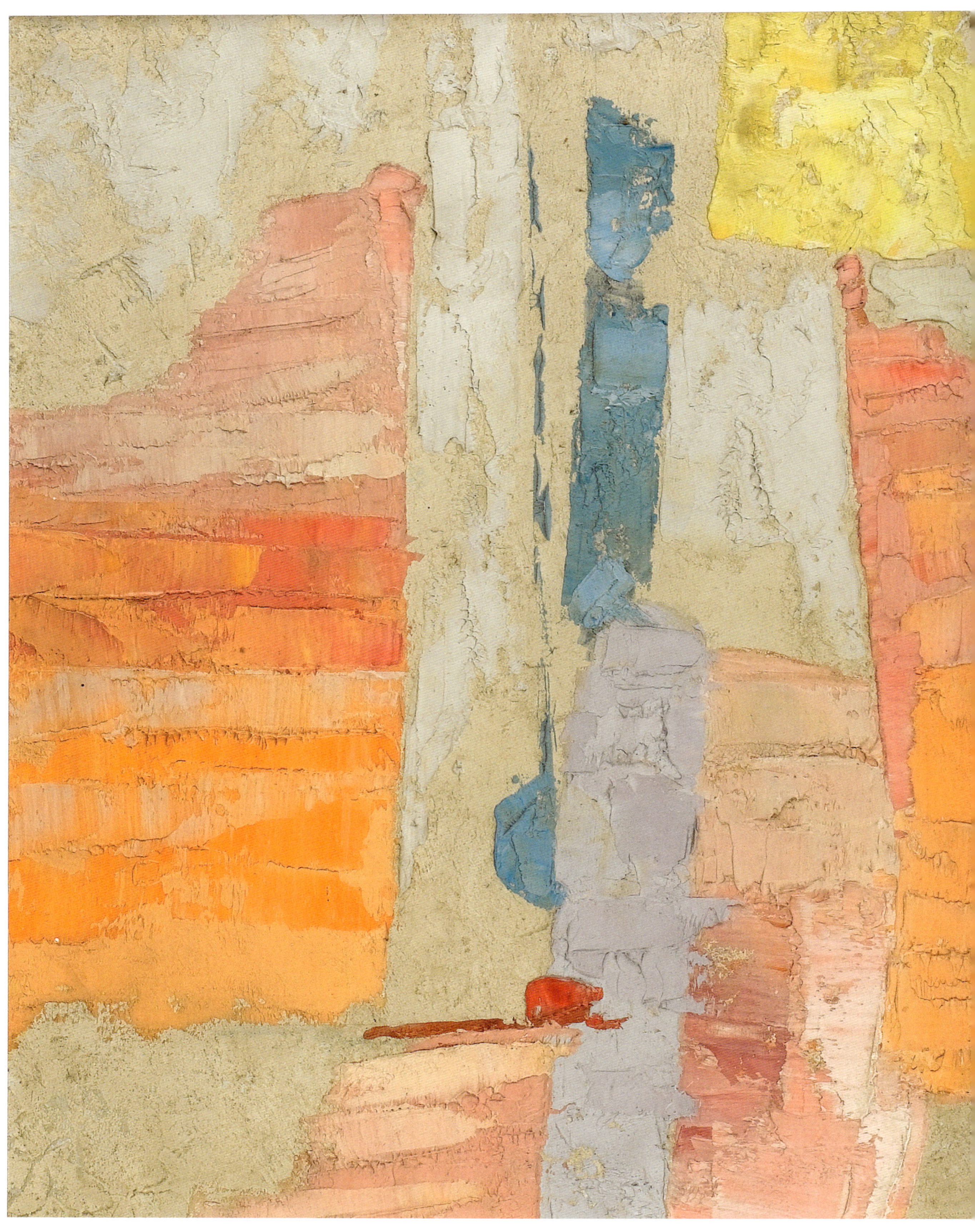

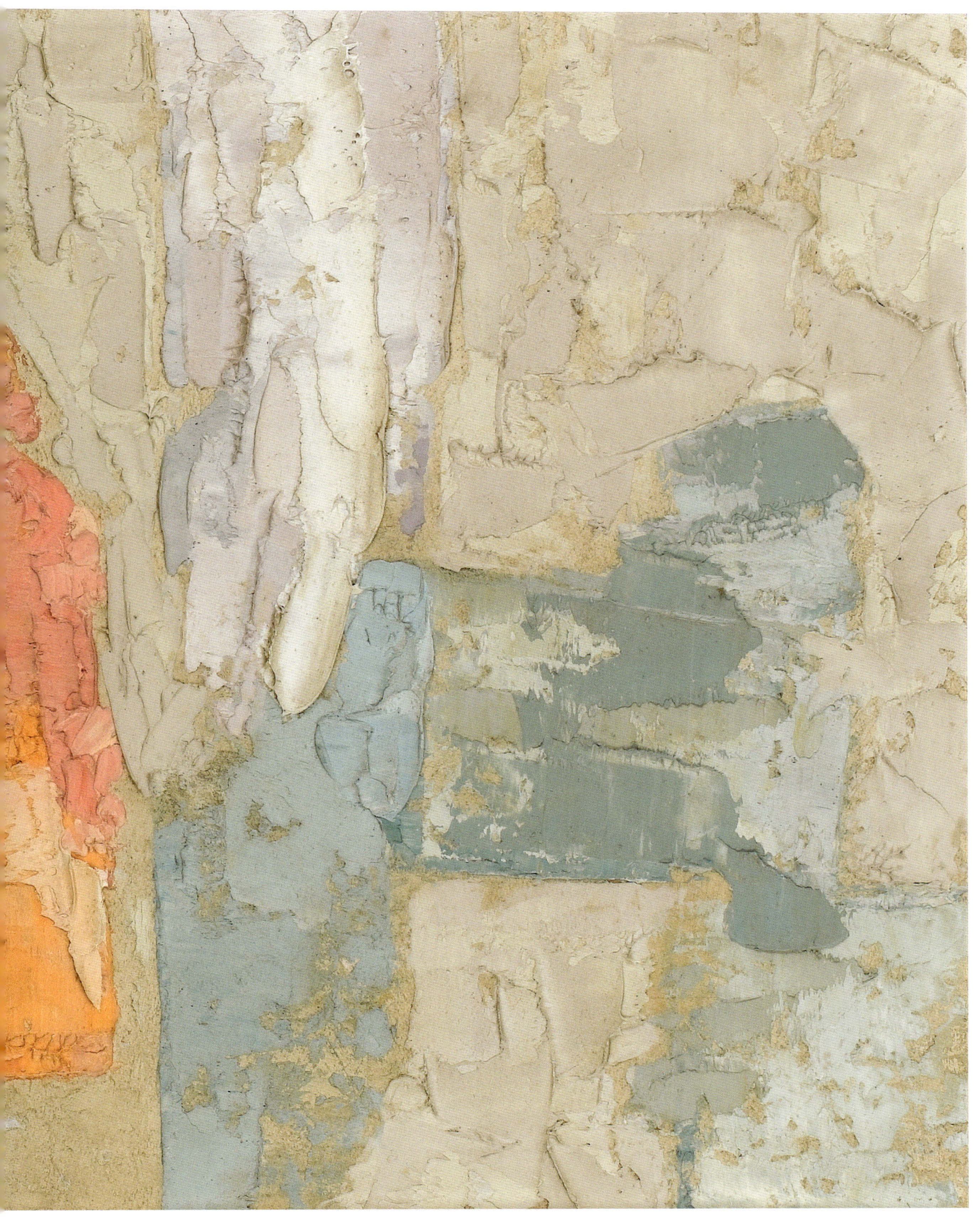

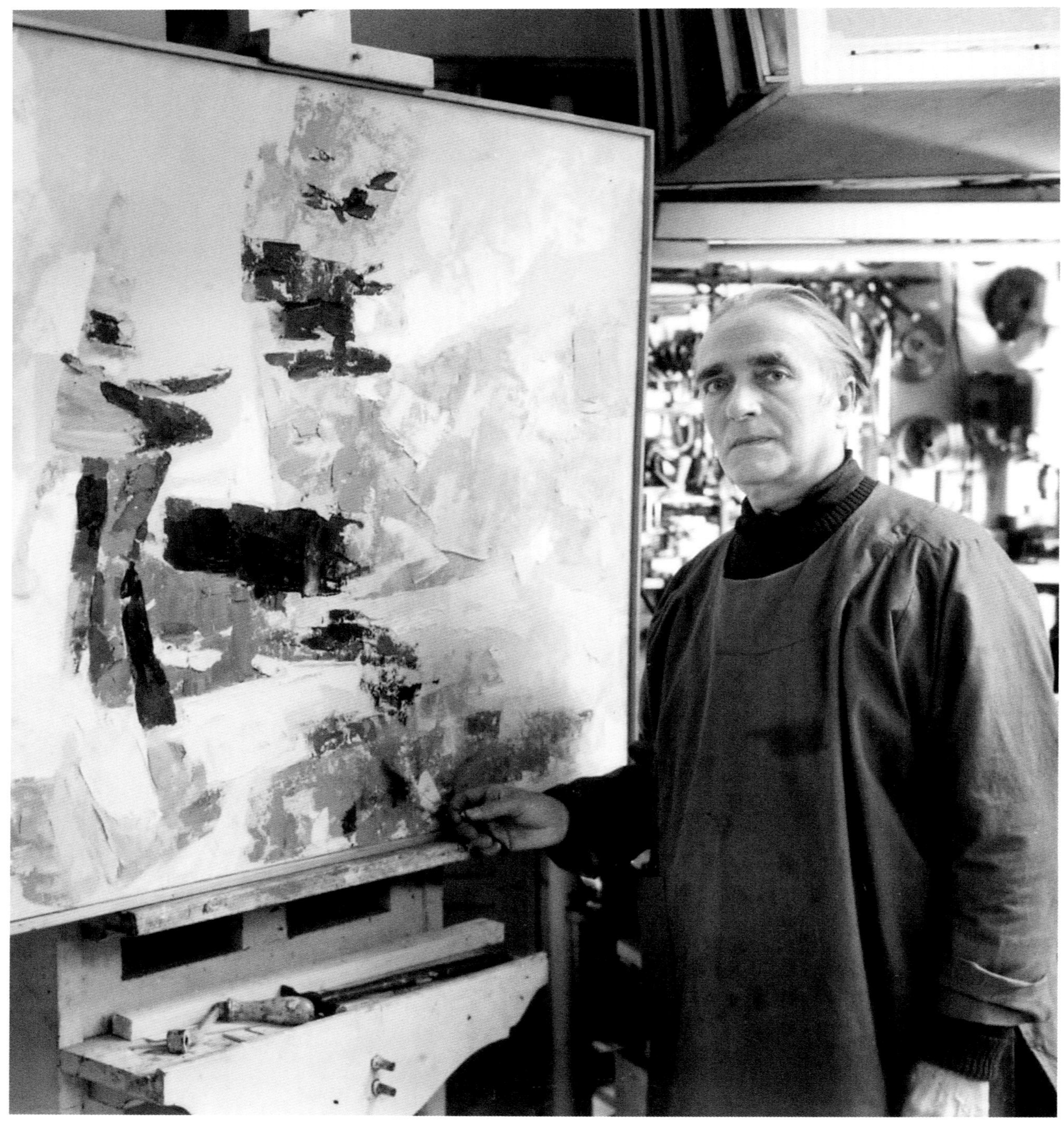

Fig. 31 – John Cecil Stephenson in his studio, c.1960.

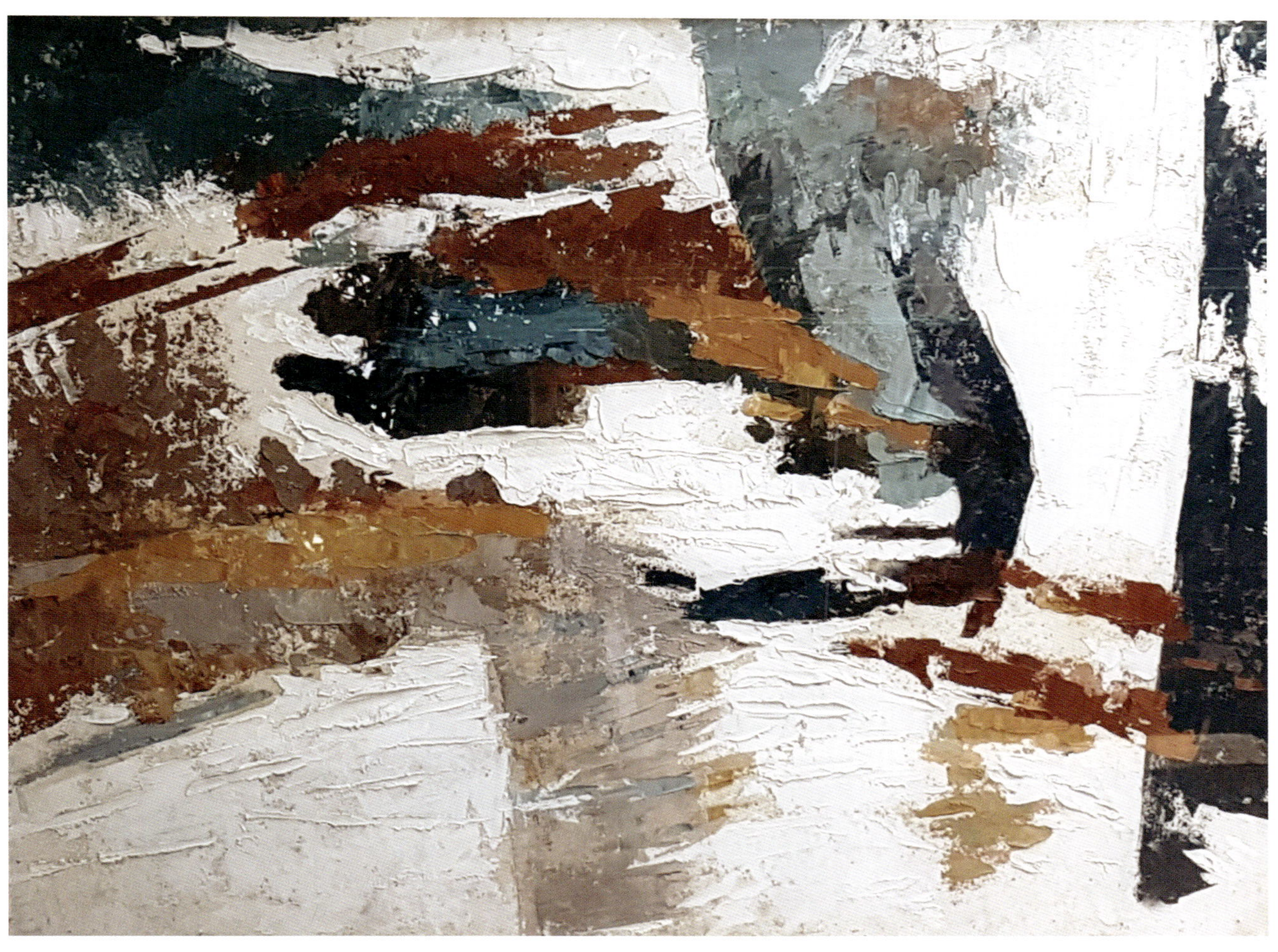

CAT. 34 – *Bravura*, 1960, signed, titled and dated on labels to reverse, oil on board, 48 × 36 in. (122 × 91.5 cm).

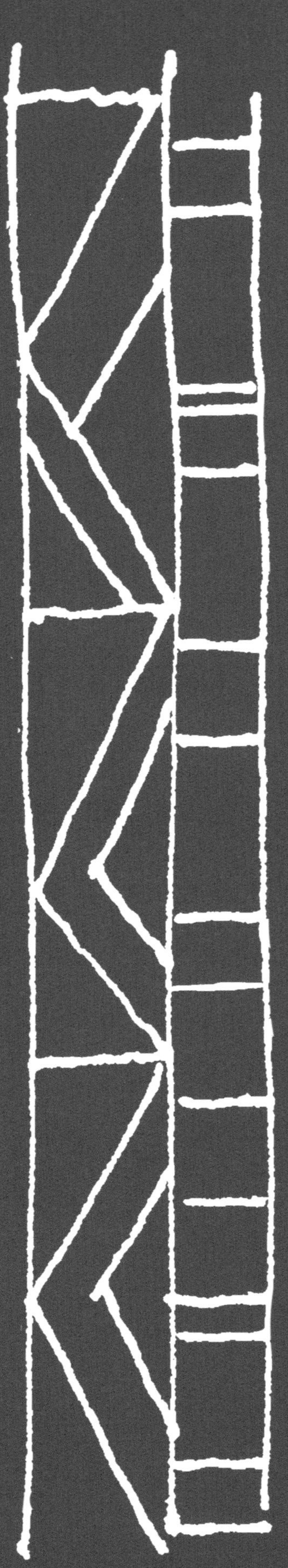

BIOGRAPHICAL NOTES

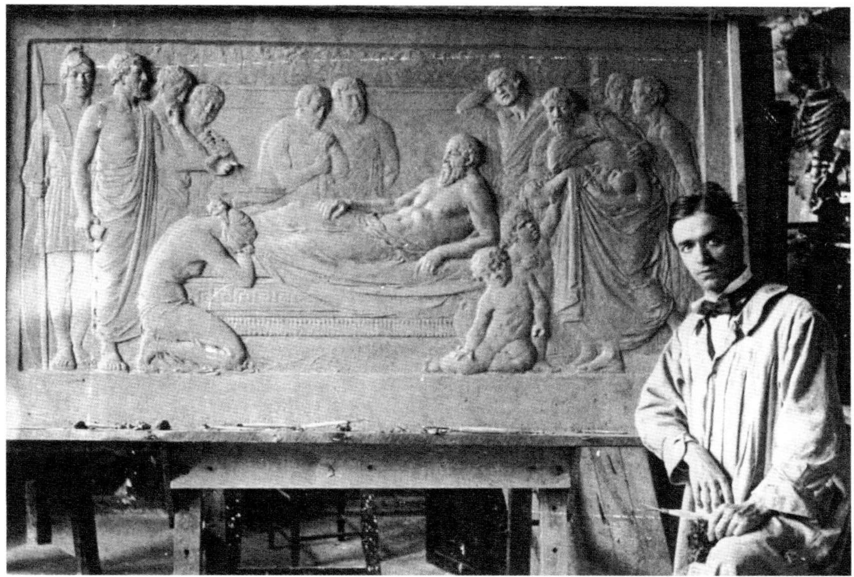

Fig. 32 – Stephenson beside a Bas-Relief 'The Death of Socrates' that he carved in 1912.

1889
Born 15 September in Bishop Auckland, Co. Durham, to Robert and Elizabeth Stephenson.
Educated Bishop Barrington School, Bishop Auckland.

1904
Wins a Scholarship to King James 1st Grammar School, which fostered his musical as well as artistic talents.

1906-8
Darlington Technical College; decides to become an art student.

1909-14
Wins a scholarship to Leeds School of Art for three years, followed by two years as a pupil teacher.

1914
Scholarship to Royal College of Art, London.
Works as a skilled hand on large lathes turning artillery gun barrels.
Meets Walter Sickert, who advises him to find a studio. Takes the lease of 6 The Mall Studios, Belsize Park, London, where he lives for the rest of his life. Paints portraits and landscapes.

1922
Appointed Head of Art, teaching in the Architectural Department, Northern Polytechnic, London; lectures
and teaches painting and drawing.

1926
Tours Italy and visits his brother, Alfred, in Paris.

1928
Tours Northern England to produce series of watercolours of Northern castles.
Barbara Hepworth and John Skeaping move into 7 The Mall Studios.
Henry Moore moves into 11a Parkhill Road.

1930
Tours Highlands of Scotland.

1932
2 January – Marries Sybil Mason.
2 October – Meets Ben Nicholson, then living in Parkhill Road.
Produces The Pump, his first abstract work, followed by a series of machine pictures in which the design possibilities of lathes and pumps are developed; from this point Stephenson develops a series of geometric abstracts exploring the possibilities of particular basic forms.

1933

Ben Nicholson and Barbara Hepworth move into at 7 The Mall Studios
Herbert Read (and new partner Margaret Ludwig) move into 3 The Mall Studios

1934

Exhibits with 7&5 Society, works include *Mask*.
Hampstead arts community was becoming a haven for refugee painters and sculptors, and JCS met new influences including Gropius, Naum Gabo and Hans Erni.

1935

Exhibits in 'Abstract Section' at the Artists' International Association, London.

1937

Leslie Martin, Nicholson and Gabo produce a book, *Circle, International Survey of Constructve Art*, essentially a manifesto of the Modern Movement in Britain, coinciding with an exhibition at the London Gallery. It included a full page illustrated by JCS, *Six Elements*. It was intended to establish the position of British Abstract Artists in the international forum.

1938

In October, the Nicholsons gave a party at N° 7 which included Fernand Leger and Alexander Calder. Calder rented a flat in Hampstead for five months, during which time he became a frequent visitor to JCS's studio.

1939

JCS divorces Sybil.
January-February – *Living Art in England*, London Gallery
February-March – *Abstract Work*, Artists International Associatio Whitechapel Art Gallery, London
March – *Abstract Paintings by 9 British Artists*, Lefevre Gallery, London. Is described as a constructivist, and one tempera is illustrated in *Living Art in Britain* catalogue, London Bulletin, published by London Gallery.
Ben Nicholson and Barbara Hepworth move to Cornwall; Henry Moore takes over lease of N° 7.
21 September – Piet Mondrian arrives from Paris with Winifred Nicholson.
Moves into a flat in Parkhill Road. For the next twelve months Mondrian and Stephenson see much of each other.

1940

No.6 Mall Studios is damaged in the Blitz, which also prompts Mondrian's departure to the USA. Is made redundant by the Northern Polytechnic (apart from fire-watching) and directed into war-work. There is very little painting.

1941

Marries the painter Kathleen Guthrie.

1942

Returns to figurative work; paintings of the Blitz are bought by the Imperial War Museum, and the Northern Polytechnic, where he is re-engaged.

1944

Works on war pictures including 'Death of a Doodlebug', first shown at the RA; also semi- abstract works based on the human figure.

1950

Returns to abstract work on a larger scale.

1951

Luminescent Ceiling Decoration in the Pavilion of Power and Production at the Festival of Britain, 10 × 30 feet, executed in fluorescent colours and illuminated by ultra-violet mercury lamps.

1956

A friend and colleague, the architect Bill Curtis, plans to build himself a pioneering 'Solar House', heated and cooled by solar panels and heat-pumps. He commissions JCS to design the hand-made iron staircase, and a large mural (10 × 8 feet). The mural later goes to Churchill College, Cambridge, and then to the USA.

1957

As a result of the Solar House, is commissioned by Ply Glass Ltd to design a series of coloured laminated glass murals for buildings in Newcastle and London, (including Engineering for the exterior of the Engineering Faculty, Queen Mary's College, London University, Mile End).

1958

185' × 13' ply glass mural for the British Industries Pavilion at Brussels International Exhibition; dismantled and re-erected at a sports stadium Hilversum, the Netherlands; Stephenson wins a silver medal for this design.
Article on pavilion and ply glass design in *Architecture and Building* magazine

1959
Canon (2), 1958, bought by the Arts Council of Great Britain.

1960
First one-man exhibition at the Drian Galleries of recent work, all with musical titles; catalogue introduction by Sir Herbert Read.
Ply glass designs by Stephenson and Edward Curtis are exhibited at the Association cf Industrial Artists.
Suffers three strokes which left him unable to move or talk.

1962
Work is reproduced in *British Art and the Modern Movement* by the Arts Council of Great Britain.

1963
Painting, 1937 is acquired by the Tate.

1964
Early abstracts are included in *Mondrian, De Stijl and Their Impact*, exhibition at Marlborough Galleries, New York.

1965
March – Early paintings in *Art in Britain 1930–40* exhibition at Marlborough New London Gallery.
August – Works are included in *Historically Important 20th Century Masters* exhibition, Drian Galleries.
Articles on Stephenson in *Architectural Design* and *Studio International* .
13 November – Dies at his home, 6 The Mall Studios.

1966
November/December – Memorial exhibition held at Drian Galleries.

1967
Work is included in *British Painting* at the Tate Gallery.

1972
Work is reproduced in *The Non-Objective World 1939–1955*.

1973
October – Four works are included in *Aspects of Abstract Art in England* exhibition, Alexander Postan Fine Art April/
May – Three works in *Hampstead Two* exhibition at Edward Harvane Gallery

1974
August/September – Three works are exhibited in *Aspects of Abstract Painting in Britain 1910–60* at Talbot Rice Art Centre, Edinburgh; and then in Brussels, November/December 1974 and Germany, March/April 1975
November – *Mechanism* and *Vortex I* are exhibited in *Hampstead in the Thirties* exhibition at the Camden Arts Centre

1975
Retrospective exhibition, Camden Arts Centre, London, touring to Laing Art Gallery, Newcastle

1976
October/November – Fischer Fine Art, Exhibition of paintings, gouaches and drawings, 1932–1957

2007
Painting, 1937, included in British Art 1900– 2007, Tate Gallery
John Cecil Stephenson (1889-1965), The Fine Art Society, London, in association with Paul Liss

2012
John Cecil Stepehnson – Pioneer of Modernism, DLI Museum & Durham Art Ga lery, curated by Conor Mullan

John Cecil Stephenson

Tony Mould

Cecil Stephenson was the Head of Art at the Department of Architecture, The Northern Poly-technic, in the Holloway Road, London N7. Known to all as 'Steamboat'. He was a short man who lived in a studio house in Hampstead, off Haverstock Hill. When He arrived on his motorbike, a large and heavy Sunbeam S7 motorcycle, he was invariably wearing a navy blue beret.

One of his frequently used words was "a propos", so I wondered if he had lived in France. Some of his friends were very successful artists. He told us that one had valuable Persian carpets, and made visitors change into the soft slippers, provided on entry to his house. Another of his friends was the American sculptor Alexander Calder (1898 – 1976), world famous as the originator of 'mobiles'. He made them from stiff wires from which were suspended counterweights in various forms. They were suspended from the ceiling and responded readily to any air movement.

At the Poly we had weekly life classes. The man who came always wore a cap. His uncut hair was coiled round inside it, in a similar way to the Sikhs. A lady of uncertain age was also a model.

As well as life drawing we were given a good grounding in colour theory and the characteristics of colour pigments. Messrs. Power and Lodge were the two assistant masters. In the studio we produced drawings of classical buildings which had to be rendered with many graded washes. The medium was usually Chinese ink, produced by rubbing the solid stick on a saucer of water. We also made frequent visits to the Victoria and Albert museum, producing coloured copies of, for example, an Etruscan fabric. Other subjects were objects in the Cast Court, such as the Trajan column. I enjoyed drawing and measuring the furniture there and based my design for a new sewing table on two eighteenth century examples. I made the table myself from mahogany, but asked the joinery teacher in the trade school on the ground floor of the Poly to machine the many vertical flutes around it. Our studios were on the first floor, above the trade school, where they taught all of the building trades, so we were able to see just how things should be done. The disadvantage of the Poly was that it was sited in Islington, opposite the Holloway Road tube station. The atmosphere in London at that time, before the Clean Air Act, was very dirty. In consequence large black smuts descended onto our sheets of expensive drawing paper. This in turn led to taking the drawing work home to do, and so to burning midnight oil. I spent one Christmas calculating the shadows cast by light switches and round fittings and then drawing them in isometric projection. The subject is called sciagraphy. Students now do not do these kinds of things, which instead are now produced by computers.

In the 1951 South Bank exhibition, Steamboat painted a mural on the ceiling of the corridor leading into the Dome of Discovery, which was designed by Ralph Tubbs. The abstract painting, sited above an unlit corridor, used special coloured paints that glowed when illuminated by an otherwise invisible ultra violet light. The effect was quite dramatic.

One of Cecil's abstract paintings, later bought by the Tate Gallery, was on sale in Heal's shop. I saw it and liked it, and asked Steamboat if he would paint me a copy. That was in 1955. The price

6 MALL STUDIOS PARKHILL ROAD LONDON N W 3

GULLIVER 2200

Sept 22 55

Dear Mould,

Your picture will be finished tomorrow, Friday; as I have to be in Hornsey Road about 10, if it is convenient for you I could bring your picture to your address, near bye. In any case, you could please 'phone me & say whether it will be alright for me to bring it on Saturday morning, or, if not, make some other arrangement.

Kindest regards to you both
Yours very sincerely
Cecil Stephenson

P.S. On second thoughts, I will bring it unless you 'phone on Saturday morning

quoted was too much for a student, so he produced a somewhat smaller one, two-thirds the size, for £60. He entitled the reduced abstract 'Divertimento II '. It consisted of flat iron shapes of differing colours on a white background, painted in egg tempera. He made the wooden frame for the painting. It, too, was painted matt white, but the narrow front edge was gilded. This was too bright for the artist's liking, so he dulled it. I still have the painting.

In 6 Mall Studios, Parkhill Road, London N3, where he lived, Steamboat had a large and comprehensive machine workshop. The road was near Belsize Park tube station, and not far from Hampstead Heath. At the time I visited his studio, Steamboat had a blacksmith's fire rigged up outside, blown by an old vacuum cleaner fan, and was making iron brackets to support an exhibit in the Victoria and Albert Museum. His second wife, Kathline Guthrie, was also a noted artist. She worked in a shed in their small rear garden, and in fact emerged from it while I was there.

John Cecil Stephenson was born in 1889. There was a retrospective exhibition of his work between 29 January and 19 February 1975, at the Camden Arts Centre, Arkwright Road, London NW3 6DG. He died in 1965, aged 76. His second wife, Kathleen Guthrie, was born in 1905 and died in 1981, aged 76.

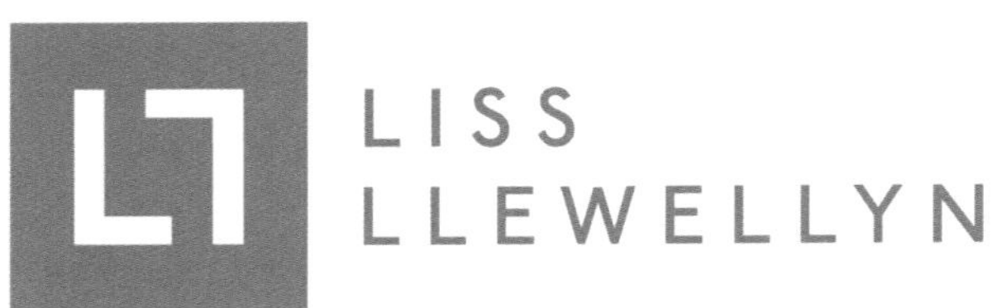

Founded in 1991 by Paul Liss and Sacha Llewellyn, LISS LLEWELLYN are fine art dealers who have worked with musuems worldwide and publish over 30 books contributing to a reasssesmet of 20th century British art.

George Richards
GEORGE@LISSLLEWELLYN.COM
+44 (0)7497 492756
Gallery Manager

Paul Liss
PAUL@LISSLLEWELLYN.COM
+44 (0)7973 613374
Director

Sacha Llewellyn
SACHA@LISSLLEWELLYN.COM
+ 33 (0)6 28 95 07 84
Director

Steven Maisel FCA
STEVEN@LISSLLEWELLYN.COM
+32 (0)4 77 23 53 12
Company Secretary

Registered Office:
Adam House
7-10 Adam Street
London WC2N 6AA

Telephone:
+ 44 (0)207 520 9225

www.LISSLLEWELLYN.COM